Transforming
the
Market

Transforming the Market

the

Market

Towards a new political economy

Patrick Diamond

CIVITAS
INSTITUTE FOR THE STUDY
OF CIVIL SOCIETY · LONDON

First Published October 2013

© Civitas 2013
55 Tufton Street
London SW1P 3QL

email: books@civitas.org.uk

ISBN 978-1-906837-58-7

Independence: Civitas: Institute for the Study of Civil Society is a
registered educational charity (No. 1085494) and a company limited by
guarantee (No. 04023541). Civitas is financed from a variety of private
sources to avoid over-reliance on any single or small group of donors.

All publications are independently refereed. All the Institute's
publications seek to further its objective of promoting the advancement
of learning. The views expressed are those of the authors, not of the
Institute.

Designed and typeset by
Richard Kelly

Printed in Great Britain by
Disc to Print
London

'The difficulty lies, not in the new ideas, but in escaping from the old ones'.

John Maynard Keynes, British economist

'The conventional view serves to protect us from the painful business of thinking'.

John Kenneth Galbraith, US economist

'The sheer scale of support to the banking sector is breathtaking. In the UK, in the form of direct and guaranteed loans and equity investment, it is not far short of a trillion (that is, one thousand billion) pounds, close to two-thirds of the annual output of the entire economy. To paraphrase a great wartime leader, never in the field of financial endeavour has so much money been owed by so few to so many. And one might add, so far, with little real reform'.

Mervyn King, Governor of the Bank of England

Contents

Author

Patrick Diamond is Lecturer in Public Policy at Queen Mary, University of London and Vice-Chair of Policy Network. He is Gwilym Gibbon Fellow at Nuffield College, Oxford, and a Visiting Fellow in the Department of Politics at the University of Oxford. Patrick is also an elected member of Southwark Council. He is the former Head of Policy Planning in 10 Downing Street and Senior Policy Adviser to the Prime Minister. Patrick has spent ten years as a Special Adviser in various roles at the heart of British Government, including No.10 Downing Street, the Cabinet Office, the Northern Ireland Office and the Equality and Human Rights Commission (EHRC) where he served as Group Director of Strategy. His recent publications include: *Beyond New Labour* (with Roger Liddle, 2009); *Social Justice in the Global Age* (with Olaf Cramme, 2009) and *After the Third Way* (with Olaf Cramme, 2012); and *Global Europe, Social Europe* (with Anthony Giddens, 2006).

Foreword

Since the 2008 financial crisis, the prevailing debate about the economy, in Westminster and the media, has been about how best to achieve an immediate return to growth. Does the economy need a Keynesian shot in the arm from the state, or is the more important priority to reduce the deficit? Some commentaries leave the impression that this debate will be more or less wrapped up by the time of the next general election, when the nation will give its verdict on the rival arguments and where they have got us. This, after all, is the primary focus of a political class that struggles to raise its sights beyond its next run-in with the electorate. As Patrick Diamond's book shows, however, this short-term perspective on the economy, driven by the demands of the electoral cycle, is naïve if not irresponsible.

What has been lost in the stimulus-*vs.*-austerity din has been the debate the country really needs about how we secure economic growth, not over the next five years but over the next 50 years. That debate is already going on, and it is acknowledged by politicians, but it needs to achieve greater prominence in the political and public arenas. In *Transforming the Market: Towards a new political economy*, Diamond provides a lucid and coherent account of the obstacles to long-term prosperity in the UK. Simply put, the economy is too reliant on financial services, on London and the South-East, on the shareholder corporation and on the twin monoliths of the State and the Market. Growth achieved without addressing these imbalances is unsustainable. Growth achieved by encouraging more private debt (witness George Osborne's support for homebuyers which has helped to re-inflate the housing market) is as a strategy akin to playing snakes and ladders with the economy.

So what is to be done? First of all, it needs a recalibration of priorities. The short-term pursuit of growth, allowing the unfettered free market to create as much wealth as possible which can then be redistributed by the Government, has led us into what Diamond calls a 'low wage, low skill, low productivity "disequilibrium"'. He acknowledges that the last Labour government – in which he served as a Downing Street policy adviser – did little to prevent that. The challenge for the present generation of party leaders is to recognise New Labour's mistake.

Drawing on a wide range of thinking from recent years, this book sets out a great many practical possibilities for change. Some are already being promoted by the Labour leadership: regional banking and a living wage, for example. The philosophy of 'pre-distribution' – seeking to secure a fairer distribution of wealth through pay packets rather than tax credits, to put it crudely – is also now part of the Labour lexicon even if there is still some uncertainty about how it should be achieved (not to mention how to explain it on the doorstep).

But there is no reason why the political economy Diamond advances should appeal only to the centre-left. The decentralisation of power to local communities, greater pluralism in the economy, incentivising long-term investment, promoting small businesses, a stronger emphasis on traditional craft skills and vocational training – these are objectives that should be shared by policymakers across the spectrum. Some of the details may provoke disagreement, but the fundamental task of rebalancing the economy, of repairing the structural weaknesses that have been so badly exposed since 2008, is one that all politicians urgently need to grapple with. Whatever the next set of growth figures looks like.

Daniel Bentley
Civitas

Summary

All political parties should be concerned with the long-term performance of the British economy, not only relative to other OECD countries, but to the emerging market economies of Asia and the east. There is great potential to significantly rebalance the British economy towards fairer, more sustainable and regionally balanced growth, investment and net trade: the automotive sector already accounts for ten per cent of UK exports and is growing steadily; Britain has world-leading expertise in the construction sector, and some of the best universities in the world as the appetite for merit goods such as education rises in the emerging market economies; there is a strong British civil aerospace sector as the demand for air travel continues to increase globally, alongside the UK's position as the world's largest e-commerce market; the opportunities for exporting UK creative and digital output are enormous, as is the potential in sectors where the UK traditionally has comparative advantage such as business services and pharmaceuticals (CBI, 2011).

Nonetheless, despite important progress in recent decades, there is still the need for 'catch up' in key aspects of competitiveness, notably education, training, infrastructure, productivity and innovation. This book proposes key institutional reforms across a range of policy arenas. The overall purpose of 'institution-building' is to increase long-term commitment and trust in an open economy. This approach emphasises the importance of institutional co-ordination as the motor of long-term competitiveness and value creation, as set out below:

Strengthening skills, the education system and vocational institutions

◆ Boosting the role of academy schools in the most disadvantaged areas

◆ Widening the network of 'second-chance' learning institutions

◆ Raising the quality of apprenticeships and improving co-ordination between firms

◆ Harnessing traditional craft skills

◆ Embedding the living wage and raising the minimum wage immediately from £6.19 to £6.60 an hour

◆ Supply-side reform to boost equity in market outcomes through 'predistribution'

A regional economic strategy and regional banking

◆ A system of local banking building on the German 'Sparkassen' model

◆ A structure of regional public interest banks replacing the national investment bank

◆ Expanding credit unions and 'peer-to-peer lending'

◆ Enshrining a British Community Reinvestment Act

◆ Rebuilding national and regional infrastructure through capital investment including allowing regional airports in Birmingham, Manchester, Leeds/Bradford, Newcastle and the East Midlands to expand, where capacity permits

Corporate stewardship: from shareholding to stakeholding

◆ Encourage long-term business investment: tapering capital gains tax on shares from 50 per cent in year one to 10 per cent after ten years; end the practice of quarterly reporting

◆ Investment and pension funds should have the same tax regime as individuals

- Raise the threshold on corporate take-overs from 50 to 60 per cent ensuring those who vote have held the shares for at least one year

- Extend employee ownership allowing workers to be partially remunerated in shares and widen the availability of profit-sharing schemes

- Emulate the 'S-corporation' model enabling firms to generate cash internally

A civil economy: pluralisation and decentralisation

- Use public procurement to diversify the economy and promote small and medium-sized businesses (SMEs)

- Build local economies from the bottom-up giving local authorities more discretionary powers

- Channel research and development (R&D) spending more effectively to strengthen innovation

- Ensure regulations and rules overseeing the Internet promote Britain's creative economy

- Extend capital allowances to promote manufacturing and the 'manu-services' sector

- Introduce NI exemptions for firms who train and up-skill workers, as well as those who improve export performance

- Create an economic 'super-ministry' at the heart of Whitehall combining the Department of Business, Innovation and Skills (BIS), the Department of Communities and Local Government (DCLG) and core Treasury functions, with a specific remit to decentralise and devolve economic power away from central government; key public institutions ought to be dispersed outside London: for example, the House of Lords ought to have a regional base; cultural institutions such as the Royal Opera House and the British Museum ought to be re-located in Northern cities.

I

Introduction

This book is intended as a contribution to the wider debate about the future of the British economy. The focus is how to 'rebalance' judiciously economic institutions and markets in the aftermath of the 2008 financial crisis, which brought to an end 47 consecutive quarters of UK growth, among the most successful periods in economic performance since 1945. The crash was followed by the most serious depression in the industrialised economies for more than a century. The post-war British disease of 'boom and bust' had not, after all, been cured. Since the crisis, economic growth in the United Kingdom has been anaemic, with widespread fears of a 'double-' or 'triple-dip' recession. There are signs of tentative recovery in the economic data, but these ought not to be overplayed: there are still many obstacles to sustained economic revival in the UK. There is talk of a 'lost decade', a sustained period of prolonged stagnation akin to Japan in the 1990s, leading to a dramatic decline in material living standards and national prosperity. As a consequence, there has been a multitude of expert commissions which have examined the case for a comprehensive United Kingdom growth strategy – from the Heseltine Review to the more recent growth report by the London School of Economics. While each has made distinctive policy recommendations, something of a *consensus* has emerged: the reviews have emphasised the role of active, enabling government in fostering national competitiveness through state-led industrial policy. This represents a subtle but important shift in the dominant view of the role of the state in the advanced industrialised economies since the 1980s.

This book will seek to question that consensus, arguing that an explicit focus on the goal of rising national income and Gross Domestic Product (GDP) as the primary objective of economic policy risks repeating the policy errors that led to the 2008 crisis. For one, there is a danger that policy-makers are attempting to resuscitate a flawed economic model, an asset-based 'balloon' economy, instead of creating the conditions for a more durable and sustainable economic model based on a fundamental *rebalancing* of the British economy. The ever-present danger of merely repeating past errors is exemplified in George Osborne's 2013 Budget announcement on mortgage finance for first-time home buyers, which seeks to revive growth in the British economy by 'pump-priming' the domestic property and housing market. The Chancellor's mortgage finance initiative, undoubtedly important as a mechanism for promoting the objective of wider home ownership, is at risk of recreating the asset bubbles that were such a powerful contributory factor to the financial crisis of 2008-9.

In addition, it is argued that focusing industrial policy solely on reviving the rate of national economic growth through an interventionist state and an increased role for conventional bank finance is unlikely to succeed. The attempt to 'force-feed the goose' by pump-priming a 'debt-financed, consumer-driven economy' (Hay, 2010: 2) through loose monetary policy will do little to tackle its fundamental structural weaknesses, as Manchester University's Karel Williams has recently attested (Williams, 2012).[1] This weakness in Britain's underlying productive potential is epitomised by data which demonstrates that the 20 per cent depreciation of sterling since 2008 has not

---

1 In the United Kingdom, property prices rose by an average of more than ten per cent a year in real terms from the late 1990s until the 2008 financial crisis.

produced any discernible improvement in United Kingdom export performance, especially in goods. Britain is now producing more motor vehicles than ever before, but on average 35 per cent of the components in British cars are *imported*. There are other embedded structural weaknesses: Britain's dysfunctional 'ecology of ownership' and the absence of a corporate stewardship culture; the slow rate of technology adaptation, absorption and innovation; stark inequalities in spatial and regional performance; and a series of 'broken' supply chains which have weakened growth potential in key sectors while constraining output.

What the British economy needs is not only a government-backed industrial policy, but a *national economic strategy*. This strategy does not merely focus on expanding GDP, but seeks to alter the composition, quality and distribution of economic growth. This alternative approach would not only address the growth deficit in the British economy: it would pursue the objective of *rebalancing* so as to emphasise the importance of stability and resilience in economic institutions and markets. The concept of rebalancing may be thrown around casually in political debate, but it has a specific rationale. The aim is to ensure that political and economic institutions are capable of addressing the inherent volatility of markets, strengthening the economy's underlying productive base and increasing the capacity for fairer and more sustainable growth. This involves action to recalibrate the British economic model across four key dimensions (Gamble, 2011):

♦   First, *rebalancing* consumption and investment in the aftermath of a perilously inflated asset bubble, combined with addressing the public/private debt overhang which continues to weaken domestic re-covery.

♦   Second, *rebalancing* between the 'financial' and 'manufacturing/high-value service' sectors in the light of concerns about the disproportionate influence of City interests on the regulatory and incentive structures of the British economy.

◆ Third, *rebalancing* regional growth, particularly between the South-East and the North-East of England, given increasing spatial inequalities between regions which recent approaches in economic policy appear to have exacerbated.

◆ Fourth, *rebalancing* the primary distribution of material living standards and disposable incomes by altering the underlying pattern of wage determination through a strategy of 'predistribution': making primary market outcomes more egalitarian.

The goal of 'rebalancing' the economy entails nothing short of a *new politics of production*. As far as possible, public policy needs to focus on promoting the dynamic production of 'high-value' goods and services, instead of generating 'speculative' value through increasingly sophisticated financial engineering. This, in turn, should aim to create a high-wage, high-skill, and high-productivity economy providing more secure jobs together with real rises in living standards, particularly for those in the lower and middle deciles of the income distribution. There is little future for the United Kingdom in pursuing a growth strategy based on further reducing the unit costs of production, since comparative advantage lies in high value-added tradable goods and services. The importance of developing a new economic model is underlined by the severity of the 2008 crisis which hit the UK more dramatically than every other industrialised economy. Output in the UK economy declined by $562 billion between 2007 and 2010. The next worst performer among the developed economies was Italy, with a much smaller decline of $65 billion.

Astonishingly, the UK's decline in dollar GDP since the crisis has been almost two-and-a-half times that of the entire Eurozone (Ross 2012), indicating the extent of Britain's exposure to global financial shocks – a further reminder that fundamental changes are needed. The emphasis on economic *rebalancing* is anchored in the political economy literature which focuses on the role of institutions and public actors in modern economies, alongside the influence of markets in shaping outcomes.[2] This envisages the purpose of economics not as predicting or shaping future events, but promoting wide-ranging debate about the diversity of policy options available in an environment characterised by what Keynes once described as 'radical uncertainty'.

The emphasis on rebalancing nevertheless reflects a more fundamental strategic rationale. The weakness of the British economy, long predating the 2008 crisis, is the lack of long-term relationships and trust embodied within political and economic institutions that foster legitimacy among economic actors. The UK is particularly adept at being flexible, adaptive, dynamic and embracing a rapid rate of change, which explains many of the sectoral improvements in growth and productivity performance over the last 30 years. The danger, however, is that the absence of *trust* and *commitment* among economic agents leads to chronic *short-termism* which explains many of Britain's long-running weaknesses: in particular the failure to train younger workers, a historically low rate of capital investment, an unwillingness to invest in innovation, and poorly developed partnerships with higher education institutions and the public sector. Adair Turner (2002) argues that British firms operate in a culture which encourages risk-averse decision-making, further depleting long-term investment in human capital, technology, plant and machinery. The

---

2 This political economy literature was particularly concerned with debates about 'varieties of capitalism' and the diversity of economic institutions within capitalist states: it is associated with the work of Andrew Shonfield (1965), Peter Hall and David Soskice's later treatise, *Varieties of Capitalism* (2001), and David Marquand's writing on the developmental state in *The Unprincipled Society* (1989).

solution outlined in the book is not to intervene so as to veto or slow the pace of economic change, but to create and sustain institutions that are capable of fostering long-term relationships, collaboration and trust. This onus on forging long-term value creation and the importance of trust is most recently elaborated in Colin Mayer's work, *Firm Commitment* (2012).

In so doing, this book explicitly challenges the dominant approach to political debate about economic policy that has recently taken shape in the United Kingdom. On the one hand, there is the argument for *traditional Keynesian stimulus*, until recently closely associated with the leadership of the opposition Labour party. The strength of this approach is self-evident in the context of a 'double-dip' recession apparently made worse by austerity measures and sharp reductions in public spending, which even the International Monetary Fund (IMF) argues have been ill-conceived and poorly timed. Leading economists from Robert Skidelsky to Paul Krugman have sought to add intellectual weight to the contemporary Keynesian case.

The weakness of traditional Keynesianism, nevertheless, is that it may risk merely reinforcing underlying structural imbalances, increasing state spending to expand the level of aggregate demand without addressing the structural pathologies that contain the seeds of the crisis. In that sense, the accumulation crisis afflicting the British economy ought to be interpreted as a *structural* crisis relating to the productive capacity of the economy, as much as a cyclical crisis fuelled by inadequate *demand*. The Conservatives in particular have adopted the metaphor of the 'public household' to argue that the answer to borrowing is not to borrow more (Gamble, 2012). There is apparently little appetite among British voters for an economic policy remedy that requires higher government deficits.

On the other hand, the *free market-orientated* paradigm favoured by the new right is similarly focused on resuscitating the pre-existing growth model. The diagnosis of the 'market fundamentalists' is that the crisis has been encouraged by excessive regulation in product, capital and labour markets, weakening the 'self-correcting' properties of markets, and escalating levels of debt and public borrowing. So, the argument goes, excessive government interference has weakened the ability of western economies to compete with low-cost producers in Asia and Latin America. Nonetheless, the new right perspective has come under serious challenge, from Conservative thinkers as well as liberals and social democrats (Norman & Ganesh, 2006). The British growth model has been weighted heavily towards the banking sector and financial services since the 1980s, stoking market 'imbalances' which have led to the erosion of manufacturing industry. This has, in turn, reinforced stark regional inequalities; the long tail of low skills and lower-than-average earnings has exacerbated what Conservative thinkers characterise as endemic 'state dependency'. For example, social security spending under the Thatcher governments reached 15 per cent of GDP due to higher levels of unemployment. Higher welfare spending since the late 1970s has itself been driven by what is arguably an imbalanced economic model.

The sense of a deepening crisis in political economy and the suspicion that neither of the conventional ideological approaches in British politics holds water has grown deeper since the crisis broke five years ago. Indeed, faith in the popular remedies of both Keynesian stimulus and market fundamentalism is rapidly receding. Moreover, it is far from clear that British governments are capable of delivering either of the policy initiatives recommended by these approaches: public spending cuts or a rapid return to growth. The Coalition government has trumpeted the radicalism of its proposals to shrink the size of the state, in particular by reducing departmental spending in Whitehall. Yet the government's plans, even if they are achieved, merely return the British state to the 40 per cent share of national income that has been in place for much of the last

30 years. In key areas such as the welfare state and social security, the Coalition has struggled to reduce spending due to the severity of the recession, as the bill for working-age benefits has soared.

In the meantime, Labour's case for a temporary increase in public borrowing rests on its claim to be able to dramatically improve growth performance through improved macro-economic management, additional supply-side reforms in product and capital markets, and a further boost to public infrastructure. However, the party's plans do not so far go much beyond the industrial policy mantra tentatively outlined by Peter Mandelson from 2008 to Labour's election defeat in 2010. Historically, Labour governments have tended to overestimate their capacity to produce a short-term increase in the rate of economic growth, as the Wilson administration's 'national plan' demonstrated in the 1960s. As a result, neither of the dominant intellectual paradigms in British economic debate – *Keynesian stimulus* nor *market-centred austerity* – offers a viable political economy strategy for the United Kingdom over the decade ahead.

The British centre-left and political economy

This debate is arguably of particular relevance to the centre-left in British politics, given the historic interest of social democracy in questions of economic growth, full employment, redistribution, social welfare, and living standards. The post-2008 crisis represented a fundamental challenge to several decades of 'neo-liberal' orthodoxy culminating in a series of bank failures, the collapse of financial markets, escalating public and private debt, and the bonus boom among City bankers. It is little surprise that a sharp turn to the left in the aftermath of the crisis has been widely anticipated. Yet despite the intellectual assault on the core tenets of neo-liberalism, the revival of the left's alternative model of political economy which apparently perished during the economic crises of the 1970s has not come to fruition, five years on from the collapse of Lehman Brothers. Instead, it is social democracy which, paradoxically, appears most devoid of ideas and governing credibility in the aftermath of the crisis throughout Western Europe.

This goes to the heart of the debate about economic competence, and the historical reputation of parties of the left for economic mismanagement which has dogged their attempt to become natural parties of government since the Second World War. Since the 2008 crisis, the centre-right in Britain, as elsewhere in Europe, has been ruthless in seeking to decouple social democracy's claim to economic efficiency from the *moral* argument for greater equity and social justice (Gamble, 2012). Whereas in the past, the left argued that economic efficiency and social justice went hand in hand, fiscal austerity enabled the Conservatives to claim that Labour's traditional commitment to fairness and a more equal society could only be achieved at the expense of economic growth and prosperity, imperilling the recovery.

This claim had credibility because centre-left parties had been in power when the crisis struck, nowhere more so than in Britain: New Labour was associated with a period of overzealous financial deregulation and an inadequate policy regime designed to ensure macro-economic stability. At the same time, the new right argued that social democracy's commitment to protecting public sector jobs and services was illusory, since they visibly lacked the means to pay for those policies in the absence of economic growth. As such, the historic claim of social democracy to reconcile economic efficiency with social justice no longer appeared credible to voters (Gamble, 2012).

In truth, an intellectual void emerged within centre-left politics, exacerbated, in particular, by the collapse of faith in the traditional 'Croslandite' model of social democracy.[3] This approach emerged in the late 1950s, broadly accepting the

---

3 As encapsulated in Anthony Crosland's seminal work on social democratic political theory, *The Future of Socialism* (1956).

reality of the market economy while repudiating the Labour party's historic commitment to the nationalisation and public ownership of the means of production, distribution and exchange which had defined its strategic purpose since the late nineteenth century. The aim of centre-left political economy after Crosland was to accept the reality of the competitive market economy, but to redistribute the fruits of growth more equitably through the distribution of public services, social security and the maintenance of a universal welfare state. This strategy shaped Labour's approach to political economy from Harold Wilson and James Callaghan in the 1960s and 1970s to Tony Blair and Gordon Brown in the 1990s and 2000s.

Nonetheless, in the intervening decades, the underlying assumptions of Crosland's model have been undermined by economic and social change. Growth in the UK economy can no longer be taken for granted, and may never recover to 'pre-crisis' levels, particularly given the long-term process of economic restructuring eastwards and the resurgence of the BRIC (Brazil, Russia, India and China) economies. Markets have been shown to be inherently unstable and 'crisis-prone'; the era of 'boom and bust' may be far from over. As importantly, high levels of social spending has meant too little thought was given to how to make the structure of the economy and labour markets more *egalitarian* in the outcomes they produced.

In hindsight, it is clear that Labour after 1997 had no concerted strategy for breaking out of the low-wage, low-skill, low-productivity 'disequilibrium' which characterised the British economy since the early 1980s. The 'Croslandite model' requires governments to redistribute outcomes that are growing ever more unequal in their primary distribution as the result of technological change, the impact of globalisation on developed economies, and reforms that have weakened the bargaining power of labour. As such, it is not sufficient for the state to be neutral about the operation of markets, altering the *post hoc* distribution of outcomes through social policy interventions. This calls into question the current balance between flexibility and security in the labour market, and the increasing importance of employment protection and regulation.

Public Interest and Political Economy

The aim of this book is to develop a strategic framework drawing on the insights of the political economy literature: an approach to economic policy that recognises the decisive role of institutions, public policy and the public interest in shaping the operation of markets (Painter, 2013). There are important historical precedents for such an approach: in post-war Germany, for example, social institutions were created that helped to re-build a competitive market economy. The literature acknowledges that the challenges facing the British economy are not merely financial and economic, but concern the impact of *politics* and the role of political and social institutions in shaping market outcomes. This approach indicates that the state will continue to be decisive in influencing the rules, regulations and incentives governing modern capitalist economies; the United Kingdom is hardly an exception. Over the last century, social democrats have adopted several distinctive strategies in economic policy: state planning; social welfare; and 'market-based' approaches (Gamble, 2012). It is likely that each of these elements will need to be incorporated in order to achieve a more equal distribution of income and wealth in the future, alongside improved growth performance.

The approach adopted is to seek to combine a politics of dynamic *production* with the politics of fair *distribution*: the goal of public policy should not merely be to share out the 'national income cake' more fairly, but to grow the cake so that all citizens can enjoy the fruits of sustained prosperity in the coming decades. The tradition of political economy draws particular attention to the importance of sustainability and the real nature of economic value, distinguishing between 'speculative' value generation, and growth based on 'real' productive value. This echoes the distinction drawn by the leader of the Labour party, Ed Miliband, between 'predators' and 'producers', and the case for a more 'responsible' model of British capitalism. Moreover, the book examines how to fundamentally redistribute economic control, a theme echoed in recent pronouncements by Red Tory and Blue Labour thinkers, including Phillip Blond and the Labour peer Maurice Glasman. As such, the book will assess:

◆ **The macro-level**: what assumptions ought to guide policy-makers in addressing the need to *rebalance* the UK economy; how can a new politics of production be refashioned in the wake of the crisis?

◆ **The meso-policy level**: what specific policy initiatives should drive rebalancing, including national and local government action that stimulates productive investment, the removal of unnecessary barriers to enterprise and deregulation, alongside measures to achieve a higher level of 'pre-distribution'?

◆ **The micro-level**: Particular attention is paid to the role of the *civil economy*: creating a more resilient and balanced economy from the 'bottom-up' through the spread of mutualism, social enterprise, decentralisation and active local government, as well as engagement with economically disadvantaged communities.

In relation to specific institutional initiatives, four key areas are highlighted as drivers of *rebalancing* the British economy:

◆ First and foremost, the need to establish genuinely world-class **vocational institutions** which provide high-quality, work-based training and skills in the UK labour market. It is not sufficient simply to embark on a further reform of the UK qualifications system: the arrangements for training and human capital acquisition have to be co-ordinated robustly between individual employees, firms, educational providers and the state. There is scope for policy transfer from other continental European countries, notably Germany and the Netherlands, which have historically achieved higher levels of *co-ordination* between the public and private sectors in delivering training and skills provision.

◆ Secondly, creating **regional banks** and **regional economic strategies** which ensure that finance flows directly to local businesses and 'niche' sectors throughout the economy. The risk of a *national* investment bank is that it perpetuates imbalances both *within* and *between* regions: London and the South-East dominate the supply of finance, but even within under-performing regions, core cities gain further at the expense of peripheral areas. The key is to endow institutions on a regional basis that can serve the interests of the whole economy, while restoring relationships based on trust and long-term commitment. The regional banks would themselves be 'public trusts', managed at arms-length from ministers and central government in Whitehall. A regional banking structure would provide an institutional anchor for regional economic policy which did not rely on simply recreating the Regional Development Agencies (RDAs) initiated by the previous Labour administration.

◆ The reform of **corporate governance** is necessary, thirdly, to ensure that businesses, particularly in the financial sector, are incentivised to create *real* value, not merely *speculative* value. This is not simply a matter of amending the existing legislative framework to abolish quarterly reporting, and to put more grit into the system to minimise predatory takeovers. Instead, fundamental cultural change in British firms is necessary both among managers and shareholders, matched by a commitment to long-term investment and value creation. This relates to the 'co-determination model', a key feature of the German system, which brings together the workforce, senior management and shareholders, sustaining an alliance for long-term productive investment, while curbing the excesses of executive pay and strengthening shareholder accountability. Shaking up the culture of British capitalism is not just about what national governments do: it is about how shareholders and economic actors discharge their responsibilities.

◆ Finally, and perhaps most crucially of all, strategies are required that can effectively stimulate the **pluralisation** of the British economy and its structures of ownership by incentivising the growth of community-based SMEs, mutuals, co-operatives, and social businesses, narrowing the divide between *public* and *private* enterprise. A plurality of institutional models would help to make the economy more resilient and stable in the wake of global shocks, instead of relying on equity-based, shareholder 'PLCs' (public limited companies). There is evidence that mutual businesses in particular give workers a greater stake in long-term value creation. Nonetheless, mutuals are hardly a panacea for solving all of our economic ills. Moreover, the strategy for pluralising the British economy has to involve further steps to advance the goal of a genuinely 'asset-based' democracy in Britain, including the wider dispersion of capital and share ownership. In addition, the absence of political decentralisation within England has to be addressed; democratically elected local leaders need the levers and powers to play a much greater role in driving local economic growth, building on recent initiatives such as City Challenge and Local Economic Partnerships (LEPs).

These approaches, firmly anchored in the long-term development of institutions, go beyond the narrow confines of industrial policy forged in Whitehall. Instead of hyper-innovation and intervention by ministers at the centre, the emphasis ought to be on shaping a long-term economic strategy for Britain to meet the goal of *rebalancing*. Since the early 1950s, industrial policy in the United Kingdom has passed through broadly two phases. The first was the approach which reached its peak in the 1970s: cultivating *national champions* in key sectors and industries. This was followed, 20 years later, by the *pro-competition* policy of the 1980s which focused on 'horizontal' interventions designed to improve long-term economic performance including investment in skills, and liberalisation of product and capital markets (Owen, 2010).

It is worth taking seriously Geoffrey Owen's insistence that errors in industrial policy stemmed historically from 'exaggerated faith' in the capacity of governments to 'identify and correct market failures' (2010: 6). It is unwise, he argues, to attempt to replace the judgement of business managers with that of government bureaucrats: industrial policy should be 'horizontal', promoting innovation and competition through markets, rather than 'vertical' and sectorally-based. Yet there are manifestly ways of seeking to shape market forces to create better outcomes for the economy as a whole which do not rely on second-guessing the corporate strategies of firms.

Moreover, Rodrik (2008) has questioned the implicit separation between 'vertical' and 'horizontal' approaches: in practice, most 'horizontal' interventions have tended to favour particular types of 'vertical' activity. For example, targeted exchange rate policies will inevitably privilege 'tradable' over 'non-tradable' sectors. According to Aiginger (2007), there are striking differences in the models of industrial strategy pursued over time and between countries, even in Western Europe. These include 'sectoral targeting' *vs.* more conventional horizontal measures;

policies to restructure large firms *vs.* the promotion of greater competition through encouraging diverse entrants, spin-offs and SMEs; competitiveness through setting the right 'framework conditions' *vs.* micro-targeting of key industries and sectors; and finally the provision of subsidies to protect existing firms *vs.* the promotion of innovation accepting the ongoing process of 'creative destruction' and technological restructuring.

Aiginger attributes burgeoning interest in industrial policy among national and European policy-makers to several factors. The first relates to the recognition that Western European countries are 'open, rather than closed' economies: there is now limited scope to protect and restructure industries through trade tariffs and state subsidies, especially for countries that remain members of the European Union. The era of national protection strategies 'incubating' new sectors and industries has almost certainly come to an end: innovation-led industrial policy which invests in growth sectors rather than protecting failing firms has grown in salience.

Secondly, most countries in Europe have largely failed to originate successful innovation policies which have the capacity to promote higher growth performance and replace moribund industries. Moreover, countries such as the UK have tended to suffer from a lack of co-ordination in 'horizontal' areas such as training and skills. This has led to information asymmetries, market failure and a loss of technical efficiency. Rodrik (2008) identifies improved *co-ordination* between sectors, industries and firms as a key pillar of modern industrial strategy. At the same time, the privatisation and deregulation policies of the 1980s and 1990s did not produce the efficiency gains that were initially anticipated, and the EU accession countries are searching for a strategic approach that does not involve the return to socialist planning. This has ensured that industrial policy is back in vogue, at least in much of the EU.

Thirdly, interest in industrial policy has revived as

there is a greater need than ever to 'soften the burden' of structural change created by globalisation and technological adaptation, leading to the widespread loss of traditional 'core' industries and jobs. Indeed, as the pace of change has accelerated in the wake of the financial crisis, more jobs in traditional sectors appear to be disappearing at a faster rate. While national governments cannot protect particular industries, they can equip the workforce to deal with the upheavals created by industrial change, managing supply-chains to minimise the impact of global restructuring on particular regions and communities (Bailey, 2012). The case for industrial policy is augmented by evidence that certain industries, notably the 'high-value' manufacturing sector, are more likely to generate secure, relatively well paid employment (Sperling, 2005). According to a report by Oxford Economics:

> A large manufacturing sector is advantageous for creating well-paid skilled manual jobs, many of which would be located in northern and peripheral regions of the UK. The large manufacturing sector in Germany is, for instance, one reason why German income is much more evenly distributed than in the UK (2010: 1).

The fourth factor underlying the growing interest in industrial policy is that national governments are more aware than ever of the need to support 'strategic sectors', particularly industries such as energy, renewables and defence. In the United States, federal government support has been crucial for the private sector: 58 out of the 100 most successful commercial products in the US market have been developed with support from the American state (Sainsbury, 2013). The evidence is that manufacturing is a particularly decisive 'strategic' sector: manufacturing industries matter since they are a powerful contributor to the trade balance; manufacturing provides an engine of growth for 'upstream industries'; manufacturing helps to extend the frontiers of technological development; and manufacturing creates positive 'spill-overs' for the 'high-value' services sector.

Finally, the European Union itself has become increasingly focused on industrial policy and 'future-orientated' growth strategies, notably through the Lisbon agenda. The 2000 Lisbon strategy established an annual growth target of three per cent per annum for the European Union, aiming for labour productivity and innovation 'catch up' with the United States through higher levels of investment in universities, R&D, innovation and science. In Britain, particularly, the case for active industrial policy gained ground as the objective of *rebalancing* has come more sharply into view since the 2008 crisis. In relation to major industrial policy differences between countries, Aiginger identifies four 'clusters' in Western Europe:

◆ *Northern Europe (Nordic)*: Industrial policy is based on 'future-orientated' investment in ICT, R&D and education; high-tech, knowledge-based sectors are a particular source of comparative advantage.

◆ *Continental (France, Germany)*: There are high levels of state aid (with the French particularly emphasising 'national champions'), together with stronger regulation in labour, product and capital markets.

◆ *Smaller Continental* (Austria, the Netherlands): There is less state aid and lower levels of investment in R&D. These countries are less 'technology-orientated' than the Nordic states.

◆ *Southern Periphery* (Spain, Greece): There is less investment in future-orientated sectors; regulation tends to be stricter with barriers to market entry and monopolies.

Like Owen, Aiginger (2007) concedes that government intervention does not always lead to optimal outcomes. There are measures undertaken under the rubric of industrial policy that are intended to slow the pace of structural change, but which can end up inhibiting necessary restructuring. 'Future-orientated' strategies can be based on incorrect information and faulty forecasting. Moreover, the cost of intervening in order to protect particular sectors and industries may be prohibitively high. This is a useful corrective to calls for poorly targeted 'hyper-intervention' by governments which may end up exacerbating underlying structural weaknesses. The role of 'industrial policy' should be to create activities with 'positive spill-overs' through embedded institutions that foster long-term commitment and trust; the maintenance of a pro-competition regulatory framework; the fostering of 'dynamic competiveness' in key sectors and industries; and creating long-term partnerships across sectors and with the workforce, encouraging support for industrial innovation and change.

'Going with the grain'

At the same time, any credible strategy for rebalancing the United Kingdom economy has to take account of major structural shifts that have occurred since the 1970s. As this book acknowledges, Britain is a particular type of *liberal market economy*: active state policies need to recognise this, where possible building on, and enhancing, existing strengths. The composition of output has shifted dramatically in favour of services since 1979, from 53 to 70 per cent of total GDP. At the same time, manufacturing output has declined from 25 to 20 per cent of Gross Value Added (GVA). The financial services sector grew at a rate of 2.7 per cent compared to an average growth rate of 2.2 per cent across the economy over the last twenty years (Oxford Economics, 2010). According to *The Times* commentator Anatole Kaletsky (2010):

> The new consensus states that Britain has an overextended and unstable financial sector that needs cutting down to size...The problem is that it is almost certainly wrong.

Finance and the business services, such as law, accountancy, and management consultancy that are natural spin-offs from buoyant financial activity, are the industries in which Britain has always enjoyed its clearest comparative advantage.

This is a strong statement of scepticism about the potential for fundamental rebalancing of the UK economy. Figure 1.2 below sets out the long-term sectoral changes in Britain's industrial structure since the 1970's:

Figure 1.2: Composition of UK employment by industry 1971-2008

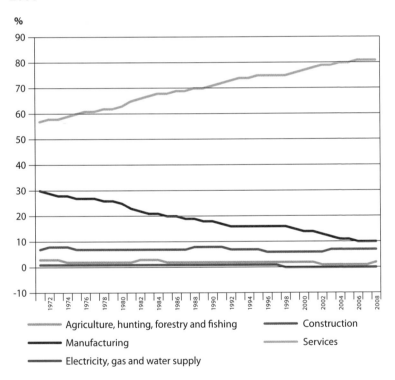

Agriculture, hunting, forestry and fishing	Construction
Manufacturing	Services
Electricity, gas and water supply	

Source: OECD Stats

In relation to jobs between 1971 and 2008, those employed in manufacturing and industrial goods production declined by 4.7 million, while employment in services rose by 10.5 million. As such, the United Kingdom has experienced significant deindustrialisation over the last 30 years; the shift towards a more service-oriented economy is broadly typical of the major industrialised countries. The stagnation of the manufacturing sector since the 1970s is, nonetheless, somewhat exceptional to Britain and has been much more dramatic than in other countries in Western Europe. This is a legitimate cause of concern for policy-makers, especially given the link between the manufacturing and service-orientated sector of the economy, captured by the importance of the *manu-services* sector. This is defined by Sissons (2011) as manufacturers combining the sale of traditional products with the development of 'knowledge-intensive' services. The United Kingdom is judged to have particular strategic advantages in the manu-services sector.

More optimistically, Crafts (2011) has argued that the century-long relative decline of the British economy ended in the late 1970s, as stronger competition in product markets led to dramatic improvements in productivity performance: immediately prior to the 2008 crisis, GDP per head in the United Kingdom was higher than France and Germany, as Figure 1.3 below makes clear. Britain became particularly adept at exploiting developments in ICT, as well as seizing the potential of globalisation and harnessing the benefits of relative economic 'openness' in world trade.

Moreover, if the goal of rebalancing is partly to address the UK current account deficit, exports in services are likely to grow faster than manufacturing, not least since ICT is increasing the tradability of services (NESTA, 2010). At the same time, there have been significant changes in the UK labour market, including a sharp reduction in trade union density, coupled with the rising Gini co-efficient for income inequality (Cobham *et al.*, 2013). The labour market has grown increasingly unequal as the bargaining power of labour has declined, fuelling rising levels of in-work poverty with adverse outcomes especially for working-age households without children. The long tail of inequality which resulted is of growing importance in political and economic debate, of concern across the ideological divide of left and right.

Figure 1.3: GDP per head of UK and comparative countries 2002-2012

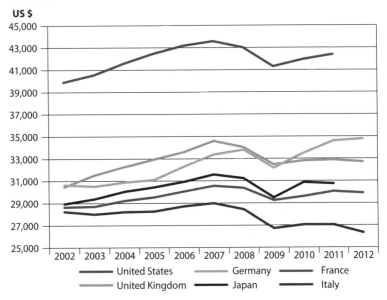

Source: OECD stats

It is clear that 'future-orientated' growth strategies will need to take account of these structural trends in the nature of the British economy and its productive base. While institutional interventions can help to address underlying structural weaknesses, active industrial strategy needs to be consistent with the United Kingdom's prospective sources of future comparative advantage. The most notable trends reshaping the British economy over the next 20 years include:

♦ A further decline in overall manufacturing output and employment regardless of the government's success in promoting key manufacturing sectors: Britain will be even more of a service-orientated economy by 2025.

♦ Potential UK growth sectors include life-sciences, hi-tech automotive and renewables, and digital industries, alongside 'high-value' services such as management consultancy, education, healthcare, law, and design.

♦ The changing shape of the UK population through demography, ageing, migration and the growth of urban populations will increase demand for new types of services and transform existing consumption patterns.

♦ The pressure on living standards is likely to continue given rising global commodity prices, and no foreseeable dramatic uplift in real wages.

♦ Britain's infrastructure needs will continue to grow, especially in digital networks, energy, waste management and transport: the Confederation of British Industry (CBI, 2011) estimate an additional £115 billion of investment will be required over the next 15 years.

♦ SMEs will absorb an ever greater share of national output and employment, and the economy will be increasingly orientated towards small and medium-sized businesses.

♦ The UK will be ever more integrated into the international economy, especially given the increasing importance of emerging markets alongside the growing purchasing power of the global middle-class.

Summary
As such, this book aims to break out of the arid and sterile ideological debate in approaches to political economy that has too often characterised public discourse in

Britain since the financial crash. At the outset, the role of active, *enabling* government is emphasised, alongside the dynamic and innovate role of markets. The legacy of post-war economic debate in Britain is a tendency to draw an artificial distinction between states and markets, rather than acknowledging that states and markets are interlinked and mutually reinforcing. The capacity to forge effective partnerships between the public and private sectors will be a crucial source of future competitive advantage. Lord Sainsbury, the former Science Minister, has made the case for an approach based on 'industrial activism' which focuses not on protecting declining industries, but on bringing the 'industries of the future' to the United Kingdom. He recognises that emerging market economies such as China are moving up the value-chain by investing heavily in Research and Development (R&D), improving the quality of public education, expanding the university sector, and developing new organisational and technological capabilities that benefit the entire supply-chain.

The approach enunciated here draws on comparative debates in political economy while recognising that countries have their own unique traditions, institutional frameworks and policy legacies that inevitably shape future choices. To contend that British policy-makers ought to transplant, wholesale, the institutions of the German social market economy to the United Kingdom is an over-simplification. As ever, it is a question of forging a uniquely *British model* drawing on the best of international experience. The choice is not between Keynes and austerity: what is required is a major programme of structural reform throughout our economy to create fairer, more sustainable and more balanced economic growth. That means acknowledging the UK's interdependence within the European and global economy, and the impact of the external environment on British economic performance.

2

The Macro-level and the New Politics of Production

The central argument of this chapter is that it would be mistaken to pursue a strategy which aims merely to re-establish the 'market-centred' economic paradigm which initially provoked the 2008 crash. The crisis was not primarily a *financial* crisis, nor has the subsequent depression been a 'normal' cyclical recession. In contrast to numerous analysts, the argument is that the crash was the symptom of a structural crisis of production in the property- and finance-driven economy that had increasingly come to dominate the United Kingdom's productive base. As such, it is a primary role of active government to fashion a renewed economic model through the process of 'rebalancing' the UK economy.

According to its critics, the 'old' neo-liberal growth paradigm predicated on the rapid expansion of financial services entailed ever greater levels of public and private debt (Gamble, 2011; Crouch, 2010; Hay, 2010). The response of policy-makers meant that firms and households have been rapidly 'deleveraging' since the crisis broke, while national governments are seeking to tackle public sector deficits, fearing a loss of confidence in the international markets. The pursuit of austerity policies has led to plummeting growth and rapid fiscal contraction in many of the advanced economies, creating serious public unrest in Southern Mediterranean states such as Greece and Spain. There is little confidence that any national economy can afford to rely on financial sector growth in the future, given the instability and uncertainty created by global shocks in international financial markets.

Over the last five years, all of the major parties in British politics have signalled their intention to develop a 'new growth strategy' for the UK economy. However, there has been less clarity about the scale and nature of the reforms required to achieve the strategic ambition. The Coalition government has emphasised its pursuit of economic orthodoxy, prioritising low inflation and public debt, 'sound money' and loose monetary policy as the primary levers facilitating a rapid return to British prosperity. In contrast, the opposition Labour party has sought to promulgate the Keynesian alternative premised on aggressive monetary and fiscal policy interventions designed to bolster aggregate demand. The emphasis within both approaches is on shoring up the old economic model, despite evidence that a more fundamental crisis of the 'mass production paradigm', which until recently defined Western market capitalism, is underway (Murray, 2009).

This book argues the case for a 'market-transforming' strategy which aims to *rebalance* the British economy, forging a new set of institutions that inculcate long-term commitment and trust (Gamble, 2012; Murray, 2009). The approach is intended to ensure significant decentralisation and a redistribution of economic power, challenging top-down, monolithic conglomerates, while opening up monopolistic markets to greater competition and contestability. The strategy for social welfare which flows from this approach emphasises the importance of dispersing 'high-value' human capital and skills more widely so as to shape the primary distribution of earnings, alongside an 'asset-based' model which gives individuals the means to withstand periodic shocks and increases their stake in the productive wealth of the economy. The purpose is to develop a diverse ecology of public and private sector institutions, including 'mutuals' and 'not-for-profit' social enterprises, which are less vulnerable to global instability and shocks. Moreover, the role of public policy should be to support and back up dynamic leading growth sectors and industries across Britain.

In an important contribution to the debate, Murray (2009) attests that the 2008 crash was not merely a crisis of the financial system, but a crisis in the 'real economy' spurred by long-term technological changes and the rebalancing of economic power from the west to the east of the global economy. Adopting the 'Schumpeterian' perspective associated with the Venezuelan economist Carlota Peretz,[4] Murray attests that crises are periods of destruction which also lead to bursts of creativity that inaugurate a new phase of growth based on novel systems of production and technological adaptation. This does not just happen spontaneously, however: existing institutions and public infrastructure have to be transformed to optimise the new growth conditions. There is clearly a strategic role for governments and public agencies.

Moreover, the process of effectively *rebalancing* the British economy requires major 'state co-ordinated' institutional reforms: the fundamental shift required is unlikely to occur if it is merely left to market forces. The task of rebalancing at the macro-level has to be engineered across the strategic dimensions alluded to in the introduction: first, rebalancing between investment and consumption; second, rebalancing between finance and manufacturing; third, rebalancing between the constituent regions of the UK economy; and finally, rebalancing between different income groups and wage earners in the British economy (Gamble, 2011). The section below will briefly deal with each of the strategic dimensions in turn.

---

4 For example, see Carlota Peretz (2002).

Investment and consumption

The extent to which the United Kingdom economy has until recently been characterised by a consumption-driven public and private debt 'bubble' has been well documented in the literature (Thompson, 2012; Gamble, 2009). UK growth has been too dependent on consumer spending made possible by cheap credit. Household and government spending have been more prominent drivers of economic growth than business investment and net trade, accentuating the imbalance between production and consumption; domestic consumption provided 89 per cent of UK GDP in 2009, greater than France, Germany and the US (CBI, 2011). The CBI report that:

> The UK's investment share of the economy in 2009 was at its lowest in 40 years and significantly lower than that of France and Germany. Furthermore, investment's *average* share of UK GDP between 2000 and 2009 (16.9 per cent) was lower than France (20.3 per cent), Germany (18.1 per cent), and the United States (18.6 per cent) and also lower than average investment share of GDP in the UK in previous decades. The UK, like the United States, has run trade deficits of over 2 per cent of GDP every year since 2001 (2011: 7).

Growth in the British economy has therefore become more unbalanced over time, despite being the most successful G8 economy in per capita GDP between 1997 and 2007. In the 1970s, 21 per cent of growth was achieved through productive investment, but this fell to 11 per cent between 1979 and 1997. In the meantime, the stock of household debt in the UK rose from 116 per cent in 2001 to 172 per cent by 2007 (CBI, 2011). Government investment has outstripped the rate of business investment significantly over the last two decades.

According to Thompson, the United Kingdom is currently the most indebted of all the advanced economies, with higher levels of public and financial sector debt than Spain and Japan. Britain's household debt is over 95 per cent of GDP, compounded by the weak household savings rate which prevailed prior to the crisis. Figure 2.1 shows the distribution of debt among the G10 economies. Britain's total borrowing, including debt held by households, governments and financial and non-financial institutions, is calculated to be over 900 per cent of British GDP. The figures for the next two indebted nations, Japan and Sweden, are around 600 and 450 per cent respectively (Morgan Stanley Research, 2011).

Figure 2.1: Debt distribution among the G10 economies in 2011

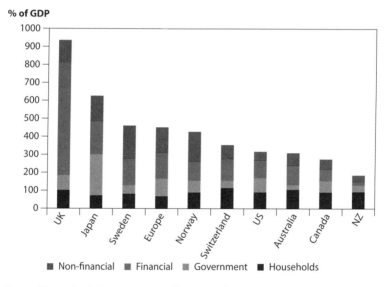

Source: Haver Analytics, Morgan Stanley research

It is the scale of Britain's banking and financial sector debt, which stands at over 600 per cent, which makes the UK's economic position so perilous. What has occurred between 2000 and 2008 is that 'declared bank liabilities' in the UK have risen by 151 per cent, leading to an ever widening gap between deposits and loans. This has imperilled the future viability of the banking sector, requiring the taxpayer-sponsored 'bail-outs' that occurred in the immediate wake of the 2007-8 crisis, prompted by the failure of Northern Rock. In relation to debt, the only 'silver-lining' has been the ability of the United Kingdom to preserve its policy autonomy through avoiding speculative attacks from foreign investors, despite other states having lower budget deficits than Britain (Thompson, 2012). That said, as Colin Hay (2010: 15-16) attests:

> The UK economy was undoubtedly peculiarly exposed... by virtue of the size, the systemic significance and the comparatively lightly regulated character of the financial sector, but it would have undoubtedly been exposed to such contagion regardless of its growth model... Moreover, and no less significantly, the sheer size of the UK financial services industry and its systemic significance for the economy and growth within it left the government with little option other than to underwrite the entire sector with public funds.

In relation to households, the level of indebtedness is a further facet of rising inequality in the affluent societies. According to Rajan (2010), western governments have dealt with the rising tide of inequality over the last 30 years by encouraging the majority of the population to 'own' housing assets and to become property owners. However, this 'democratisation' of property ownership has been achieved largely by 'debt-financing' through cheap global credit and an expansion of bank balance sheets. This attempt to compensate for growing inequality through wider home ownership has further tilted the orientation of the United Kingdom economy away from long-term investment towards destabilising credit-fuelled consumption and growth.

The need to 'rebalance' the rate of investment and the rate of consumption in the British economy relates to the emerging debate about environmental sustainability, the limits to current patterns of material affluence, and the richer debate emerging about the various dimensions of human well-being. While shifting to a strategy of 'zero growth' appears politically unfeasible given the on-going divisions between 'rich' and 'poor' both within the developing world and among the advanced economies, there is emerging agreement across the ideological spectrum that it would be desirable to rebalance the British economy away from consumption towards more long-term, 'environmentally sustainable' investment and growth (Norman & Ganesh, 2006). While this would potentially require a fundamental shift in personal lifestyles and behaviour, a sustainable investment model would act as a source of renewed economic dynamism, promoting 'green and sustainable growth' as an element of strategic comparative advantage for the United Kingdom.

Finance and Manufacturing

Arguably the most significant dimension of rebalancing relates to the relative size of the financial and manufacturing sector in the United Kingdom. In the early 1970s, the service sector accounted for 54.6 per cent of gross value-added (GVA) in the UK economy, compared to 37.9 per cent in manufacturing and construction. By the late 2000s, services accounted for 78.4 per cent of the total compared to 16.9 per cent for construction and manufacturing (CBI, 2011). The growing orientation of the British economy towards financialisation and finance-driven speculative growth is believed to be the product of the regulatory regime adopted by governments after 1979. First, the Thatcher administration encouraged the expansion of financial services by adopting a preferential tax regime, and initiating the 'big bang' that liberalised finance and capital markets after 1986. As Hay (2010: 6) has shown, the Financial Services and Building Societies Act (1986) led American investment banks to set up 'mortgage lending subsidiaries' in a rapidly expanding retail banking sector based on heavily securitised mortgage debt.

Then, after 1997, New Labour sought to create the conditions for the 'great moderation': a period of sustained economic growth driven by the adoption of a 'light touch' regime in the financial services sector. The Labour government created a tripartite system of financial regulation incorporating the Bank of England (BOE), the Financial Services Authority (FSA), and the Treasury (HMT). The post-1997 reforms have been the target of voluble criticism, not least because the tripartite structure was seen to confuse responsibility for macro-prudential regulation, while obscuring which actors were ultimately accountable for ensuring protection against systemic risk in the banking system (Daripa *et al.*, 2013).

Nonetheless, the more fundamental criticism of the post-1997 model was that the financial system was allowed to grow too large relative to the size of the economy as a whole. There was an under-appreciation of the serious decline in Britain's manufacturing position: the decrease from 30 per cent to 12 per cent of total employment is unprecedented. While the manufacturing sector's importance has been declining across the industrialised countries since the 1970s, the extent of the collapse was far greater in the UK than in other comparable economies (Oxford Economics, 2010).[5]

In considering the long-term imbalance between finance and manufacturing, Gamble (2011) has observed that many developments in British post-war political economy are characterised by path dependency. As such, they are shaped by past policy decisions and strategic choices. For example, the policy preference of British governments since

---

5 Oxford Economics (2010) notes that the decline over the past decade may in part reflect the outsourcing of services such as recruitment, catering, cleaning and accountancy which had they been done in-house would be classified as manufacturing, but which are now counted as business services.

the 1950s to defend the value of sterling and to maintain a 'strong pound' had a significant impact on the viability of key manufacturing sectors. The relative weakness of the apprenticeship system and vocational training in recent decades has similarly sapped the strength of British manufacturing industry.

As a result, the financial sector grew to be increasingly dominant over industry in the United Kingdom, further exacerbating regional inequalities. Financial services recently comprised more than ten per cent of UK national income, a higher level as a proportion of GDP than almost any other western industrialised economy. In 2011, the financial services sector contributed 9.4 per cent in gross value added to the British economy. This provided 1.1 million UK jobs, 3.4 per cent of the total workforce. The banking sector still contributes around 7.4 per cent of total tax receipts in the United Kingdom, including income tax and national insurance contributions (Maer and Broughton, 2012). The growth of the UK financial services sector in the decade preceding the 2008 crash is illustrated in Figure 2.2 overleaf.

The relative size of the financial services sector raises an important strategic question for UK policy-makers: reforms which have sought to reduce the scale of the United Kingdom financial sector through imposing a division between 'retail' and 'investment' banking activities, for example, would have an immediate, and potentially negative impact on the short-term rate of growth. This has remained largely anaemic, even stagnant, five years on from the crash, although there are indications the UK might be turning a corner.

Martin Weale from the National Institute of Economic and Social Research (NIESR) has warned that it remains 'most unlikely that the financial services industry can in the future act as the sort of motor of growth that it has done in the past... GDP is likely to be reduced permanently by about 1.9 per cent' (Weale 2009). This view is endorsed by Coutts and Rowthorn who argue that, 'global finance will become more regulated, more conservative, and less profitable than in the past' (2009: 12). As finance declines, it is likely that business services will contract further alongside continuing decline in the output of North Sea oil and gas: the widening current account deficit will compel GDP growth to slow, maintaining the rate of unemployment at a higher level than in the recent past (Oxford Economics, 2010).

Figure 2.2: GVA performance of financial services 1997-2008, index: 2010 = 100

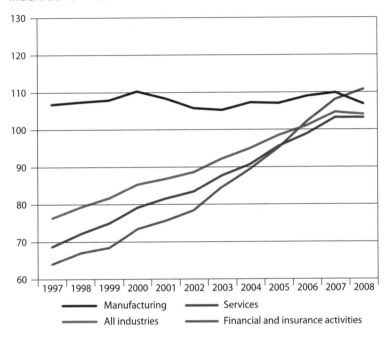

Source: ONS

As such, the process of rebalancing away from finance towards manufacturing and 'high-value' services will, in all likelihood, be slow and laborious, and may lead to unforeseen consequences, potentially weakening employment and living standards in the South-East of England (Thompson, 2012). British policy-makers, nonetheless, have little choice but to seek to adjust the banking sector's overall strategic importance. Andrew Haldane (2012) at the Bank of England has shown how the rapid growth of the banking sector since the mid-1990s led to a remorseless expansion of bank balance sheets. Ironically, this increasingly acted as a barrier to long-term economic growth, diverting human capital, assets and investment away from other productive sectors and activities towards speculative finance and banking.

This was the case in relation to 'R&D-intensive' businesses which are the motor of any dynamic, value added and knowledge-based economy. The recent flood of scientists, mathematicians and economists into the financial services sector in Britain has been well documented, skewing the allocation of highly skilled labour towards activities associated with speculative financial engineering. Within the banks themselves, the role of providing loans to individual customers and businesses increasingly became of secondary importance, displaced by 'high volume' activities including derivatives-trading and risky practices of financial intermediation. To return to this model of 'financially-driven' growth would, in all likelihood, pose a renewed threat to the stability and resilience of the British economy in a period where states generally lack the capacity to carry out further, large-scale public 'bail-outs' of ailing financial institutions.

In charting an alternative approach to financially-orientated growth, the Coalition government has set out four primary ambitions in its growth strategy for the United Kingdom:

◆ To create the most competitive tax system in the G20

◆ To make the UK 'one of the best places in Europe to start, finance and grow a business'

◆ To encourage investment and exports as the route to a more balanced economy

◆ To create a highly educated workforce that is the most flexible in Europe and able to compete with the rest of the world (BIS, 2010)

As a consequence, the government's approach is predominantly 'market-orientated': the Coalition's strategy is designed to remove the barriers to enterprise and to restore the dynamism of the market economy. Policy measures since 2010 included deregulation of the planning system; a reduction in corporation tax; a review of the tribunal system and the current system of equalities legislation by Adrian Beecroft; the introduction of tax reliefs to encourage investment and innovation; and area-based programmes including the new 'City Challenge', Local Enterprise Partnerships (LEPs) and 'enterprise zones', initiatives discussed in detail below.

These policies emphasise the importance of enabling markets to work freely in generating growth, businesses and jobs for the United Kingdom. There are similarities with much of the 'supply-side' agenda of the 1980s and 1990s, albeit with greater emphasis on the importance of skills and human capital in taking on the global competition. The Coalition government has sought to highlight the importance of capital investment in public infrastructure as a pro-growth strategy, underlined by measures in Budget 2013. Nonetheless, critics have suggested that the British government still lacks many of the instruments and policy tools that are necessary to stimulate an 'export-driven' recovery, and has been forced to rely on spontaneous growth driven by the private sector (Portes, 2012; Skidelsky, 2011; Gamble, 2011). There is an onus on active growth measures, but predominantly centred on 'horizontal' interventions such as investment in training, employability and reform of the UK tax system. In contrast, 'vertical' strategies which target particular sectors and growth industries are deemed to be emblematic of 'old-style', 1970s industrial policy.

In addition, the Coalition government's approach potentially ignores factors highlighted by economists such as John Mills (2013), who have drawn attention to the consequences of an overvalued exchange rate for Britain's export performance, particularly damaging to manufacturing industry. The 'trade-weighted' exchange rate for sterling was 20 per cent higher from the mid-1990s as the UK had deregulated capital and consumer debt markets, and large capital inflows appeared from surplus OPEC countries, notably China; this further encouraged the boom in finance and the expansion of the City of London (Oxford Economics, 2010).

The overvaluation of sterling allegedly decimated Britain's industrial base in the 1980s and 1990s, alongside the ongoing effects of global economic restructuring. Mills points out that while sterling has depreciated by more than 20 per cent since 2008, exports have grown by only two per cent. This is a disappointing performance given widely shared expectations of an 'export-driven recovery', although there is evidence that export orders are now increasing at a faster rate (Davies, 2013). In fact, continuous uncertainty about the exchange rate appears to have created a weak environment for business investment.

As such, the data suggests that Britain's overall balance of payments position has actually worsened since the financial crisis, although there have been some recent indications of improvement. Hay (2010) compares Britain's position unfavourably with Ireland: despite a severe recession and the bursting of its over-inflated property market bubble, Ireland has been able to rapidly improve its balance of payments position since the crisis; the United Kingdom, in contrast, has not. Figure 2.3 overleaf vividly demonstrates the inadequacy of Britain's current account position.

At present, the UK has a trade surplus in services, but this has been undermined by the deficit in goods since the early 1980s. By 2010, the surplus in services of £58.8 billion was outweighed by a goods deficit of £98.5 billion, an overall deficit of £39.7 billion or 6.8 per cent of GDP (CBI, 2011). According to Coutts and Rowthorn (2009), an ongoing current account deficit has tended to lead historically to lower GDP growth and currency devaluation. This is particularly problematic for the UK given the reliance on oil and gas imports, and the rising price of energy, food and commodities; it is imperative to increase the competitiveness of export sectors.

Figure 2.3: UK balance of payments since the financial crisis

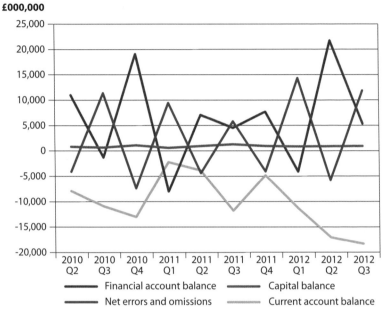

£000,000

Source: ONS

The weak rate of productive investment in Britain must account, at least in part, for such poor export performance in recent years. This is the result of both significant credit tightening since the financial crash, and the weak condition of the public finances which has largely precluded sustained capital investment by the public sector. As criticism of the Coalition's 'market-orientated' policy approach has mounted since 2010 in the face of anaemic growth rates, the government has sought to introduce additional measures such as improving access to finance, stimulating entrepreneurship, widening the availability of apprenticeship programmes, and increasing strategic investment in infrastructure (HM Treasury, 2011). Whether any of these measures has the potential to fundamentally 'rebalance' sectoral development away from finance-driven growth towards manufacturing and high value-added services, nonetheless, remains an open question for the UK economy.

It is widely acknowledged that rebalancing will be an arduous path to pursue, especially given that the United Kingdom lost more than 15 per cent of its manufacturing capacity during the last recession in the 1990s. Alan Reece (2011) calculated that Britain's manufacturing output fell by £3.5 billion a year in real terms between 1997 and 2008, which has led to a permanent loss of capacity in the supply chain and the need to import more components: rebalancing is best achieved by seeking substantially to increase the production of goods, food and energy for the domestic market in order to address the long-term weakness of Britain's balance of payments position. The United Kingdom's manufacturing base is simply too fragile to anticipate an immediate, overnight revival.

Nonetheless, it is likely that the priorities for policy-makers will continue to be supporting export-driven growth; widening access to bank finance; and improving the supply and quality of the workforce (Bailey, 2012). Strengthening the UK's current account position will depend on the competitiveness of the service sector, as well as improvements in key manufacturing industries: Britain fell behind Germany and the United States in the late nineteenth and twentieth centuries as those economies delivered significant productivity increases alongside a major shift of employment into services. Today, Britain has further to go in advancing the 'servicisation' of its economy (Oxford Economics, 2010).

As has been noted, given the depreciation of sterling since the 2008 crisis, the United Kingdom's export performance has been far from impressive. This raises serious questions about the British economy's underlying productive potential which reinforces the case for systemic rebalancing through institutional reform rather than short-term, ministerial 'hyper-intervention' from Whitehall.

Regional inequalities

Having addressed structural imbalances concerning the rate of investment and industrial composition, another obvious area for *rebalancing* relates to regional economic performance. The growing regional imbalances in the British economy over the last 30 years have been well documented. The causes of the growing divide between London and the South East on the one hand, and the North-East and North-West of England on the other, in terms of growth, employment and living standards, have been much debated among policy-makers. A report by the Prime Minister's Strategy Unit in 2001 inferred that the 'North-South' divide was something of a fiction: what mattered were the differences *within* regions, for example between 'core' cities and 'peripheral' towns, rather than the differences *between* regions. This is an important point, but it ought not to obscure the fact that significant regional inequalities have continued, resulting from wider imbalances in the United Kingdom economy.

As the British economy has become less orientated towards productive investment and more weighted towards consumption, shifting away from manufacturing towards financial services, so the extent of regional inequality has grown over the last 30 years. The manufacturing sector in the Northern regions is too modest to maintain living standards, requiring fiscal transfers from Southern England: 'This is a drain on public expenditure in the south and contributes to an unbalanced Britain' (Oxford Economics, 2010: 1). In reality, the activist regional policy adopted by the previous Labour government between 1997 and 2010 was not sufficiently robust to counter the underlying shift in the balance of economic activity towards those regions where financial services are the dominant sectoral activity. Since the 1990s, the countervailing pressure on regional imbalances has been the creation of banking jobs in the Northern regions, in particular through the growth of 'call centre' operations; alongside the significant increase in public sector jobs, particularly in the National Health Service, local authorities and the education sector, as public expenditure significantly increased in real terms after 1998-99.

Private sector growth in the North-West and North-East regions was significantly less impressive over this period; nonetheless, the 2008 crash rapidly eroded the pillars of regional economic growth that did exist. The dramatic contraction of the financial sector led to the loss of many banking jobs which had been created in the regions. Moreover, the retrenchment in public spending after 2010 led to declining employment and real wages in the public sector, having a disproportionate impact in Yorkshire and Humberside, the North-East and North-West of England. Coalition government ministers argue that jobs in the public sector are being replaced by jobs in the private sector, as depicted in Figure 2.4 overleaf, although the evidence is somewhat contested.

Moreover, researchers from the University of Manchester have shown the extent to which regional income and output disparities have grown in the United Kingdom since 1979: the three most weakly performing regions (Yorkshire and Humberside, the West Midlands, and Wales) have each slipped ten points on measures of Gross Value Added (GVA) compared to London (Froud *et al.*, 2013). As a consequence: 'All three of these declining regions now have output per capita that is less than half that of London, and if we extrapolate past trends, their per capita output could be around one-third that of the London level by 2029' (Froud *et al.*, 2013: 2). Figure 2.5 on page 43 illustrates changes in disposable income between regions over time, demonstrating how far the North-East, North-West, and Yorkshire and Humberside have slipped back relative to London and the South-East between 1995 and 2008.

Figure 2.4: Changes in UK public and private sector jobs between March 2013 and March 2012

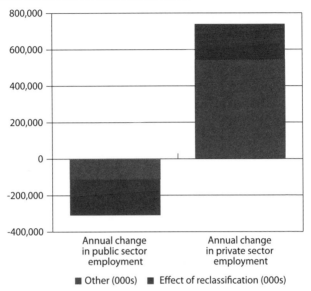

Source: ONS

The dramatic growth of regional inequality over the last 30 years is usually explained in relation to the steady shift of economic activity away from manufacturing and heavy industry, off-set by the expansion of relatively low paid and insecure public sector jobs in the social care sector and the National Health Service, which still account for 35 per cent of the total workforce in the North-East of England.

This has prompted an important debate about how to make regional economic growth outside London and the South-East more sustainable, so as not to exacerbate the strategic advantages already enjoyed by the South of England. The most powerful symbol of an imbalanced economy is geographic and spatial inequality; particular regions become congested and over-populated with inadequate infrastructure while other regions continue to decline in relative terms with far higher levels of worklessness and 'supplicant' populations at risk of permanent marginalisation. If the regional divide were to get worse, this would represent an ominous future for Britain's economy and society.

Figure 2.5: Regional gross household income per head 1995-2008, index: UK = 100

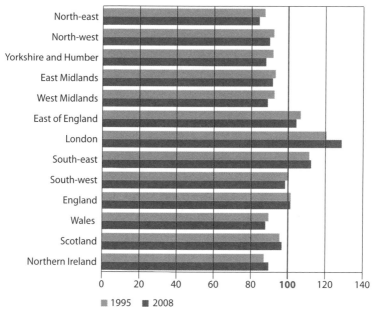

Source: ONS

Household incomes, inequality and the 'squeezed middle'

The cumulative impact of imbalances in consumption and investment, manufacturing and finance, and between the 'core' and 'peripheral' regions, is growing economic and social inequality in the United Kingdom since the late 1970s. After 1979, the share of income taken by the very top has increased three-fold, as wages have declined while profits and dividends have experienced a long boom (Lansley, 2011). The widening of wage and income inequality has been extensively documented, as has the subsequent impact on levels of child poverty and social mobility in Britain. The intractable nature of poverty and household income inequality is particularly striking given that the previous Labour administration enacted a number of measures to improve living standards for lower and middle income groups, while reducing levels of poverty among the most disadvantaged, especially pensioners and children (Lupton, 2013).

The Labour government in the United Kingdom between 1997 and 2010 sought to affect the distribution of household disposable income through mechanisms such as tax credits, increases in benefits for pensioners and families with children, and 'welfare-to-work' programmes. However, the Labour administration was struggling against the weight of structural forces which conspired to make the difference between households and regions ever more extreme over time. Since 2010, inequality appears to have worsened across the industrialised countries according to the OECD, in particular among younger families and women, partly as a consequence of the disproportionate impact of austerity policies. Indeed, there are economists who explicitly attribute culpability for the 2008 financial crash to rising income inequality (Rajan, 2010; Krugman, 2009). The importance of financialisation led to rewards for the very wealthy growing more unequal, while the median wage share shrank even further (Lansley & Reed, 2013).

The inequity of outcomes is not only an issue facing those at the bottom of the income distribution, but relates to the ongoing 'squeeze' on lower and middle incomes which appeared to begin in the early 2000s but has recently accelerated. Figure 2.6 illustrates this.

According to the Institute for Fiscal Studies (2013), the dramatic fall in median incomes in the United Kingdom over the last four years has been the largest since the mid-1970s, as mean incomes have declined by 7.2 per cent. The Office for Budget Responsibility (OBR) have indicated in their latest forecast, published alongside Budget 2013, that real earnings will continue to fall up to 2014-15, as earnings growth still disproportionately benefits higher-income households (OBR, 2013).

Figure 2.6: The position of low- to middle-income households in the working-age income distribution: UK 2010-2011

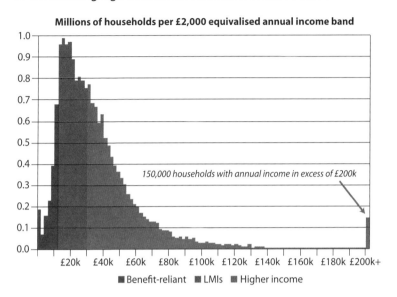

Source: Resolution Foundation/Department for Work and Pensions

The solution to rising economic inequality partially lies in correcting the wider imbalances already alluded to: between consumption and investment, manufacturing and financial services, and between the regions, in particular through improving the supply of secure, well paid jobs in the British economy. It is the structural character of the economy and the power relationship between labour and capital which leads to inequality, as much as changes in taxes and benefits over time. Recent experience has demonstrated the constrained capacity of the welfare state to address underlying structural inequalities generated in the labour market. It follows that policy-makers have to alter the primary distribution of material living standards and disposable incomes, adjusting the underlying pattern of wage determination through an agenda of *predistribution*, as outlined by the Yale political scientist, Jacob Hacker (2011).

The process of rebalancing the British economy is

necessary to ensure that the errors which led to the 2008 crisis are not repeated, while forging a more sustainable and cohesive economy. Less inequality in earnings, reduced dependency on low pay, and a higher overall wage share will create the most propitious conditions for sustained recovery (Lansley & Reed, 2013). This imperative of achieving a rebalancing of household incomes reflects a concern about the overall legitimacy of the capitalist system. Where outcomes and inequalities become too extreme across time, the stability of the market economy is imperilled. It is striking that Christine Lagarde, Secretary-General of the International Monetary Fund (IMF), argues that 'excessive inequality is corrosive to growth; it is corrosive to society... the economics profession and the policy community have downplayed inequality for too long' (Cited in Lansley, 2011: 14). Greater attention to overall levels of economic inequality may be one of the beneficial long-term legacies of the 2008 financial crisis.

Summary

There are a number of sceptics who argue that neither the previous Labour Government nor the current Coalition government had the far-reaching strategy required to bring about the much needed restructuring of the British economy (Portes, 2012; Skidelsky, 2011). There is a deepening sense that the political system itself is in crisis: none of the major parties has a repository of ideas that can offer a convincing road-map to economic and social reform. Most politicians are apparently content to operate within familiar territory of 'business as usual', returning as quickly as possible to the pre-2008 growth model which is most likely to achieve immediate political and electoral success.

As a consequence, there has been too much emphasis on the self-correcting properties of markets on the right, and the magical powers of government intervention on the left. There has been too little attention given to how the state and public institutions have the capacity to alter the underlying distribution of economic incentives alongside markets (Sainsbury, 2013; Gamble, 2011; Hay, 2010; Hutton, 1996). One of the most compelling critiques of the previously dominant 'neo-liberal' approach to industrial policy has come from an unlikely quarter, the former Science Minister, Lord Sainsbury. The Labour peer has made the case for a new progressive political economy predicated on the view that while market capitalism is necessary and irreplaceable, the system functions best when it is shaped by state-driven reforms and the guiding hand of active government.

Lord Sainsbury's argument recognises the central importance of *public institutions*, in particular the role of the state in ensuring that institutions address underlying conflicts and safeguard the public interest; and the importance of social justice in ensuring stronger economic performance, for example through investment in education, skills, knowledge, and human capital. The key institutions are financial and labour markets; corporate governance and the regulation of the firm; vocational skills and training; and the system of technological innovation (Sainsbury, 2013). Alongside other reformers, Sainsbury advocated a process of long-term institutional restructuring which cannot be left to markets, based on an activist, *state-led industrial strategy*. There is increasing evidence that other industrialised countries have been successful in promoting export-driven growth and the expansion of advanced manufacturing sectors through activist measures (Rodrik, 2008).

The dilemma for the United Kingdom, however, is that recent history means that Britain lacks many of the political and economic institutions that are necessary to promote state-led innovation and industrial policy (Gamble, 2009). The 'state-led' approach is defined by two vital elements: the ambition and scale of strategic intervention which is envisaged; and the resources towards strategic investment which are committed by national governments (Gamble, 2011). There are few policy-makers who disagree about the necessity of investment in *horizontal* interventions: public infrastructure, skills, productivity, human capital and so on. However, the 'state-led' approach advocates direct strategic investment by government *vertically* in key sectors, rather than leaving such investment decisions wholly to the market. While this may be redolent of a 1970s approach predicated on 'picking winners', active strategic investment by the UK government was used in the defence sector throughout the 1980s and 1990s. Moreover, it has for many decades been a feature of supply-side policies in the United States, operating as a key driver of technological innovation in the American economy (Sainsbury, 2013; Mazzucato, 2013).

While UK government investment in science has expanded significantly over the last decade, the capacity for scientific research is not yet of a depth and scale that is likely to produce a major rebalancing towards advanced manufacturing industry. This relates to the role of the City of London, which has been perceived as 'crowding-out' industrial investment through the dominance of financial sector interests and the maintenance of an artificially high exchange rate (Williams, 2012). The alternative model to a finance-driven economy is apparently to be found in Germany, the European powerhouse of high growth, high productivity, high skill investment and growth.

Nonetheless, Britain does not have many of the institutions that are integral to the German model such as 'co-determination' between employers, shareholders and the workforce at the level of the firm. In the 'Varieties of Capitalism' literature, Germany is classified as a 'Co-ordinated Market Economy' (CME) rather than a 'Liberal Market Economy' (LME) (Hall & Soskice, 2001). Moreover, the German model is underpinned by a 'consensual' political settlement, reinforced by a voting system based on proportional representation which has historically tended to reinforce long-term policy decisions. More tellingly, Germany appeared to become more unequal as the consequence of the 'Agenda 2010' labour market reforms which were considered necessary because of Germany's weak growth performance at the end of the 1990s.

Unquestionably, if Britain were to become more like Germany, this would entail major 'tax and spending' choices and a fundamental reform of the labour market and corporate governance. A more credible and realistic approach is to advocate a British model of political economy which draws on best practice in other states, but goes with the grain of existing British traditions and institutional practices. Models of capitalism tend to be deeply rooted and ingrained in particular national cultures and institutional histories (Hall & Soskice, 2001). The emphasis is not simply on producing the quickest possible rate of UK economic growth, but strengthening the underlying resilience of the UK economy, and its capacity to withstand exogenous global shocks. There is an acknowledgement that in a liberal market economy, growth can never be delivered directly through the state.

As such, the strategic challenges outlined here suggest that the role of national governments in the economy is likely to expand in the decade ahead: not in terms of *dirigiste* intervention in markets, but in forging public institutions that uphold long-term commitment, collaboration and trust. The nature of government's role is likely to be diverse and wide-ranging, rather than being the direct owner of state industries or the monopoly provider of public services:

◆ The government is an *enabler*, directing strategic investment to growing sectors and firms, providing fertile conditions for entrepreneurship.

◆ The government is a *regulator*, managing the inherent volatility and instability of markets, while promoting competition in product and capital markets.

◆ The government is an *equaliser*, ensuring the supply of public goods and human capital helps the least advantaged, while ensuring the distribution of household income accords with basic principles of fairness and social justice.

◆ And the government is an *innovator*, promoting experimentation, technological adaptation, alongside the discovery of new markets, services, and the advancement of knowledge.

The following section documents how the process of 'rebalancing' the UK economy might be achieved across four key areas of institutional intervention. The overall purpose of institution-building is to increase long-term commitment in an open economy which, as Colin Mayer (2012) has argued, tended historically towards flexibility, adaptability, volatility and rapid turnover in markets. Britain's public policy approach was traditionally focused on promoting flexibility and adaptability, making it relatively easy for firms to shift strategy on a whim, for example by shedding costs and reducing the rate of business investment. This made UK firms agile and dynamic, but neglected the importance of institutional co-ordination as the generator of long-term competitiveness and value creation, the most persuasive explanation for the historic British 'disease' of relative economic decline: a long tail of low productivity, low skills, low investment and rising inequality rooted in a culture of liberal *laissez-faire* capitalism which all the political parties have implicitly upheld.

3

A Programme for Institutional Reform

The recent London School of Economics Growth Commission concluded that the United Kingdom has numerous assets and competitive advantages which ought to leave it relatively well positioned in the global economy. These include a trusted and world-renowned legal system, flexible labour markets, relative openness in trade and product markets, and world-class higher education institutions, together with the capacity to serve as a trading 'gateway' to continental Europe. Over the last two decades, moreover, Britain has appeared to reverse its relative decline, enjoying the fastest rising per capita GDP among the G7 economies until the 2008 crisis.

Nonetheless, the UK has major structural weaknesses that long predate the 2008 crash. The fundamental imbalances already alluded to cannot be ignored or underplayed. There is a persistent legacy of short-termism, alongside a failure to carry through long-term investment decisions. There is a lack of co-ordination between leading economic actors, particularly between employers and educational institutions in relation both to skills, and innovation. The adversarial nature of the political system has led to too many short-term fixes and insufficient long-term, strategic decision-making with a clear policy rationale. The civil service in Whitehall generally lacks private sector skills and management experience, having lambasted industrial policy in the past as merely concerned with corporatism and 'picking winners'.

Moreover, economic growth was characterised by rising inequalities, and has not been sufficiently inclusive. The goal of public policy should not merely be growth in per capita GDP, but a measure of fairness and social justice combined with environmental sustainability. Capitalism attains legitimacy when rewards are seen to be fairly achieved and there are not gross inequalities between the lowest and highest paid earners. The long tail of inequality over the last 30 years has created a culture in the United Kingdom which is weak on long-term investment in skills and human capital, especially for those in the bottom third of the education system. This has been exacerbated by ailing public sector infrastructure, especially in energy and transport; a climate of lower-than-average private investment; and an under-developed system of technological innovation. As a consequence, there has been a low rate of productivity in key industries and sectors combined with weak export performance.

The central conclusion of this book is that Britain urgently needs a *national economic strategy*, as would be taken for granted in most major continental European economies. A national strategy encompasses, but is ultimately more ambitious than, industrial policy *per se*. Industrial policy involves 'measures taken by governments to bring about industrial outcomes different to those if markets were allowed free rein' (Owen, 2010: 4). This may include support for fledgling businesses and industries, the modernisation and upgrading of existing enterprises to meet competitive challenges, and the creation of strategic 'national champions'. Owen (2010) warns against industrial policies that inhibit the 'creative destruction process' which he regards as a key driver of improved productivity performance in the United States: it is essential that incumbent firms should be replaced by new ones, and that resources are able to move quickly to fast-growing sectors. The success of the American model is not just about the role of government intervention in fostering technological innovation (Mazzucato, 2011), but access to bank finance, the dynamism of markets, and the impact of pro-competition policy.

Nonetheless, the extent of the structural challenges facing the United Kingdom arguably goes much deeper than lack of competition in product and capital markets. There are long-term systemic weaknesses confronting the UK economy, including climate change, threats to sustainability, rising energy and commodity prices, demographic imbalances between Western Europe and the developing world, and ever starker regional inequalities (Meadway *et al.*, 2011). As such, this book argues for an institutionalist *market-transforming strategy* rather than an incremental shift towards an active industrial policy. Market-transforming strategies address the underlying productive potential of the economy: that is, the *culture* of the market economy and its institutions rather than just the immediate economic outcomes it produces.

This chapter sets out how such a strategy might be achieved through four key institutional interventions: upgrading the *vocational training and skills system*; expanding *regional banking and local finance*; reforming *corporate governance* structures to enhance long-term performance; and political decentralisation to sow the seeds of a more localised *civil economy*. There is a renewed emphasis on the role of political and economic *institutions*, since 'capitalism is a socio-economic system where institutions are key' (Sainsbury, 2013: 85).

The role of public and private institutions is to support markets, regulating who can participate, determining the rules of legitimate market exchange, defining rights and obligations, while upholding contracts and preventing fraud. The state has a key role in managing the forces and pressures unleashed by globalisation and maximising the comparative advantage of nation-states. This does not entail a return to 1970s corporatism and 'picking winners'. The international evidence indicates that the dynamic institutions of enabling government, rather than the heavy handed levers of centralised 'command and control', are most likely to produce the fastest rate of growth and economic development (Sainsbury, 2013).

I. The vocational training system and pre-distribution

The first major institutional innovation concerns the education system, skills, training and the acquisition of human capital. Since the 1970s, the orientation of UK skills policy has shifted from a 'vocationally-orientated' system built around particular sectoral and craft specialisms, towards a 'generalist' system which focuses on preparing individuals for the new global economy with the aim of constantly updating their skills and human capital. This was judged to be best suited to the institutional configuration of the UK economy which is viewed as more 'Anglo-American' than 'Northern European', a liberal market economy rather than a co-ordinated continental European economy (Hall & Soskice, 2001). Britain lacked the corporatist structures and institutions required to promote long-term investment in human capital through formal co-ordination between firms, sectors and trade unions. In recent decades, the aim of policy has been for those with higher levels of educational attainment to enter the university system, hence the 50 per cent target for university entry established by the previous government after 1997. The 'other 50 per cent' have been encouraged towards attaining various generalist vocational qualifications.

In retrospect, this approach can be regarded as a plausible attempt to fashion a skills strategy that was compatible with the British model of political economy, going with the grain of the United Kingdom's heightened orientation towards 'low' and 'high' value service industries. Moreover, one of the notable successes of public policy since the mid-1990s has been the increasing numbers of young people participating in post-16 education, partly aided by initiatives such as the

Educational Maintenance Allowance (EMA) which gave support to low-income households where pupils remained in full-time education and training. Nonetheless, there were a number of deficiencies in this generalist education and training model. A recent review by Professor Christopher Husbands from the Institute of Education has identified six key weaknesses which have emerged in the United Kingdom education and training system over the last twenty years:[6]

◆ First, *the enduring divide between 'academic' and 'vocational' education*: only 54 per cent of young people enter an academic pathway, but the alternative routes are often poorly funded and of low value in the labour market, while there has been little attempt to provide hybrid academic and vocational ('technical') training options.

◆ A reflection of the weakness in the present system is that *a fifth of vacant posts in the UK economy cannot be filled due to skills shortages*. This reflects skills surveys which suggest that young people lack requisite competencies in areas such as literacy, numeracy and communication skills. Moreover, over 40 per cent of workplaces in the United Kingdom lack 'structured training programmes' and there is an absence of sectoral co-ordination involving trade associations, chambers of commerce and trade unions. This relates to the fundamental importance of the partnership between the individual employee, business, civil society and the state in acquiring and investing in skills.

◆ Third, *increasing fragmentation between educational providers*, especially between schools and further education (FE) colleges, weakened the outcomes delivered by the education system.

---

6 Husbands chaired Labour's policy review (2013) on skills.

◆ Fourth, there has been *persistently poor quality provision within the further education (FE) sector,* despite the fact that more than one-third of A-levels are taught through FE colleges. There are particular problems relating to the teaching of mathematics, and weak links between colleges and industry. The casualisation of the FE sector and the move towards annual budgeting determined by student demand makes it ever harder to recruit and retain the best teaching staff in further education.

◆ Fifth, *the skills system in England and Wales has failed to develop sufficiently high-quality apprenticeship programmes.* Indeed, too often apprenticeships are seen as the equivalent of GCSE qualifications, rather than A-levels and university degrees. The most high-quality and well-funded apprenticeship programmes tend to be clustered in traditional male-dominated sectors, while provision in the social care and services sector is often weak. There are unresolved questions about whether apprenticeships are fundamentally about equipping young people with generic skills suited to a fluid, rapidly changing labour market, or whether apprenticeships ought to be focused on the promulgation of occupationally specific skills.

◆ Finally, *the availability of careers advice is often of poor quality,* and many careers services remain overly focused on the academic 'gold standard' route, rather than advising students on work-focused and vocational options.

Beyond these criticisms of the English skills system, as Wolf (2012) and De Waal (2009) have noted, many of the vocational qualifications that were made available have proved of dubious worth to the individual: some qualifications were poorly perceived by potential employers, having a negative impact on employability rates. This partly reflected the enduring problems of 'quality' and 'access' in the UK further education sector. The skills system has major weaknesses in relation to technician-level skills, and in STEM (science, technology, engineering, maths) subjects (Sainsbury, 2013). There have been far too few young people studying engineering, science and maths-related subjects, while there is an urgent need for technicians in growth sectors such as oil production, gas, electricity, pharmaceuticals, manufacturing and the chemicals industry. At present, Britain ranks eleventh out of 30 OECD countries in acquiring 'higher' skills, but only twentieth on the development of 'intermediate, technician-level' skills.

Another weakness of the previous approach was the failure to recognise that the purpose of the skills system is not merely to advance economic growth, but to promote individual autonomy, independence and self-worth by preparing people for progression towards esteemed, high-skilled jobs which given them a real stake in the economy and society. The danger of the British model of post-compulsory education was that it failed to encourage and reinforce personal responsibility or promote the dignity of work. This was, in part, because the post-1997 Labour government combined an emphasis on generalist vocational qualifications and labour market flexibility with tackling poverty through a system of tax credits and income support: career progression, job advancement and skills acquisition were less important since the individual would always be protected from poverty by state subsidies to the employer through the tax and benefits system. Whereas Nordic countries such as Sweden and Denmark invested three per cent of GDP in activation and re-skilling policies for the labour market, the UK invested less than 0.6 per cent between 1997 and 2010. The legacy was a growing population of households 'in work' but also living in poverty, without the realistic possibility of career development.

Finally, despite obvious institutional differences, British policy-makers have been too pessimistic about replicating the strengths of the skills system in other Northern European economies. As has been argued, institutions cannot be transported neatly from one national context to another. However, this does not mean lessons cannot be transferred and implemented across different contexts. It has been argued, for example, that employers would never invest sufficiently in apprenticeships in a liberal market economy such as the United Kingdom, since they feared 'poaching' by other companies. This could have been overcome, however, with a more sectorally focused approach, since particular firms and sectors would be more amenable to co-ordination through institutions such as the Sector Skills Councils (SSCs). Moreover, measures such as a *training levy* on employers in a particular sector would have ensured an adequate level of investment in skills programmes.

However, the greatest challenge facing the United Kingdom skills system has been the increasing numbers of young people leaving school who lack the requisite skills to succeed in work and life. Recent studies have highlighted the paradox that high levels of youth unemployment are coinciding with employer surveys which indicate a shortage of 'critical job skills' in the labour market: a global shortfall of 85 million higher- and middle-skilled workers has been predicted by 2020 (McKinsey, 2013). Figure 3.1 opposite illustrates the growth of young people not in education, employment or training over the last decade.

The inadequate levels of literacy, numeracy and social competency make acquiring advanced skills in the workplace harder and leave the individual vulnerable to a life of permanent marginalisation on a carousel between casual work and benefits. Any reform of skills policy therefore requires additional efforts to upgrade and modernise primary and secondary education, especially in England and Wales where too many pupils attend schools in which performance is still considered 'inadequate' after a decade of sustained investment and reform. Britain suffers particularly from the long tail of educational underachievement, reinforced by growing educational inequalities: for example, a fifth of children on free school meals do not reach the required standard in maths by age 7 (LSE Growth Commission, 2012).

Figure 3.1: Numbers of young people aged 16-24 not in education, employment or training 2001-2011

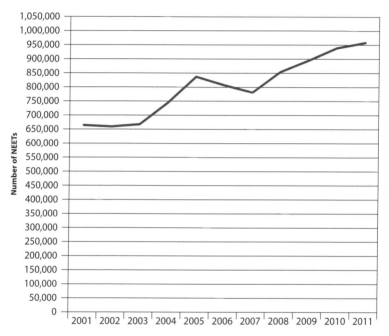

Source: Department for Education

While there has been considerable progress over the last decade, particularly in London state schools, the performance of the most disadvantaged children has improved only very slowly. School choice remains inadequate in areas where there is chronic failure; the inspection and performance management framework does not focus attention across the ability range; and too often, additional resources have failed to reach those children from low-income households. These weaknesses in educational performance are major impediments to future growth in the United Kingdom.

Secondary school reform

There is no obvious panacea for driving improvements in the secondary school system. The LSE Growth Commission proposed the creation of a more open 'ecology' of academy schools that can raise standards faster in the most disadvantaged areas. Le Grand (2007) among others argues that the most efficient way to drive up standards is to combine greater school autonomy with more freedom for successful schools to expand, ensuring parental choice within a robust accountability and inspection framework. The expansion of newly sponsored academies should be focused on schools and geographical areas with the highest proportion of disadvantaged pupils, however, combined with measures to lever up teaching standards and recruitment, as well as increasing resources for the poorest children through an expansion of the 'Pupil Premium'.

'Second-chance' schools

In addition to driving improvement in secondary education, there is a need for investment in a new generation of 'second chance' schools funded in partnership with the private sector. The model of 'second-chance' schools was initially developed by the European Commission in the White Paper 'Teaching and Learning: Towards the Learning Society' (1995). Second-chance schools are intended to provide training for young people who lack the skills necessary to enter the job market, and cannot be re-integrated into the formal education system (European Commission, 1995). They were created as non-traditional institutions geared towards social innovation, supported by each country's Ministry of Education and shaped by the local economy and educational environment. Initially, pilot schemes were established in Germany, Denmark, Spain, Finland, France, Greece, Italy, the Netherlands, Portugal and Sweden, as well as the United Kingdom. The particularities of each second-chance academy are dependent on local and national circumstances. However, some general characteristics are important:

◆ There is a committed partnership with local authorities, social services, the voluntary and community sector, and the private sector, in particular with a view to offering possible training places and jobs to students.

◆ A teaching and counselling approach is adopted focused on the needs, wishes and abilities of individual pupils, and the stimulation of active learning on their part.

◆ There are flexible teaching modules allowing a combination of basic skills development (numeracy, literacy, social skills) with practical training in, and by, public and private enterprises.

◆ There is a central role for the acquisition of skills in, and through, ICT and new technologies (European Commission, 1995).

Second-chance schools only accept those whose attendance at school is no longer compulsory. While no upper age limit has been set for entry, in practice the age of 25 has been used as a common ceiling for admission. However, what is important is that these schools are potentially vital institutions in advancing the politics of second chances, preventing individuals from slipping through the net and being vulnerable to a life-time of marginalisation and exclusion from the employment market.

The post-compulsory skills system
It is widely acknowledged that the United Kingdom has long suffered from inadequate performance in intermediate, as well as basic level, skills. There has been a significant increase in apprenticeships since the early 2000s, but these tend to be in low-wage, low-skill occupations mainly targeted at those under 25 years of age. The recommendations of recent inquiries into apprenticeships have been to get more employers involved by giving them a greater role in design-

ing the content of training, devolving a higher proportion of the skills budget, while also retaining the option to impose an industry-specific training levy (Wolf, 2012; Steedman, 2010). There ought to be measures to improve information about the availability and employability benefits of apprenticeships, and programmes need to be of higher quality with much greater focus on acquiring basic skills such as literacy and numeracy. There is also an opportunity to build on the strengths of 14-19 *university technical colleges* specialising in technical subjects and combining academic and practical skills, sponsored by major universities and employers.

No doubt such reforms would help to strengthen the British apprenticeships system. However, there ought to be greater focus on *building long-term commitment* through the skills system among educational institutions and employers. Wolf (2012) has alluded to the tendency of central government to 'micro-manage' the skills system from Whitehall, leading to an amorphous array of qualifications and educational institutions in the UK system combined with a strong element of long-term policy instability. Moreover, the skills system has to function in an economy where large employers are allegedly a thing of the past: there are fewer than 2000 factories in the UK employing more than 200 people; 75 per cent of manufacturing employment is in companies that employ fewer than ten workers. The training and skills system should be tailored to the reality of an economy increasingly built on the growth of micro-enterprises, SMEs and entrepreneurship.

Craft guilds

Nonetheless, there are aspects of the traditional skills system that ought, where possible, to be cultivated. The emphasis in Blue Labour thinking, for example, has been on how to recreate the culture of medieval 'craft guilds' that was at the heart of G.D.H. Cole and R.H. Tawney's conception of Guild Socialism in the early twentieth century. The Blue Labour account of a functioning economy explicitly rejects the onus on transferable skills in a 'free-floating' knowledge-driven economy that shaped the previous Labour government's agenda, underlining the importance of vocational skills anchored within particular traditions and histories. While it will be challenging to recreate these vocational customs in their previously existing form, the approach provides a useful corrective to skills programmes that are overly focused on inculcating generalist capabilities. There are still myriad craft industries in the United Kingdom, from software programming to traditional food production. At the same time, the focus on trade and the dignity of labour relates to the importance of fair wages and employment conditions.

The Living Wage and fair employment

The steadily rising number of minimum-wage level jobs in Britain is not a sustainable employment solution for any economy. The focus on breaking out of the low-wage, low-skill and low-productivity trap in the British economy has largely focused since the early 1990s on skills policy. However, it is also important to consider what should be the basic minimum threshold in the labour market beneath which no individual should be allowed to fall. The national minimum wage (NMW) in the UK is currently set at £6.19 an hour, combined with an array of tax credits for low-income families which are currently being scaled back by the Coalition government. The organisation London Citizens has called for a living wage of £8.55 an hour, which is what a family of two with children in London need to be able to acquire the basic necessities of life.

The living-wage campaign is not a demand for greater legislative action by the state, however. London Citizens has emphasised the importance of brokering specific agreements with employers, pressurising them to ensure 'just' pay rates for contract cleaners working in the City of London. It may also be necessary to pursue a sectoral approach to the living wage in order not to create higher unemployment among vulnerable groups with very low skills (Kelly, 2012). That said, the real value of the national minimum wage should be restored immediately by raising it to £6.60 per hour (Lansley & Reed, 2013). The living wage, accompanied by measures to increase the density of unionisation in casualised sectors, is intended to address Britain's over-reliance on the tax credit economy. This alludes to the pre-distribution agenda which is increasingly positioned as the Labour party's over-arching idea for the future of the British economy and the welfare state.

Pre-distribution and contributory welfare

There has been renewed interest across the political spectrum in the strategy of pre-distribution. According to Jacob Hacker, the purpose of pre-distribution is: 'to focus on market reforms that encourage a more equal distribution of economic power and rewards even before government collects taxes or pays out benefits' (Hacker, 2011). Pre-distribution's rationale is to structure markets in order to bring about fairer economic outcomes, rather than relying on *post-hoc* redistribution through the welfare state and 'tax-and-spend' approaches. Hacker's approach involves an implicit critique of the traditional Croslandite model of social democracy, which uses the surplus generated by private sector growth to invest in public services and the welfare state. The traditional social democratic model is an ameliorative approach under which the state compensates for the effects of the market in driving inequalities. In a world where state capacities are increasingly under pressure through fiscal austerity and reduced public spending, however, the traditional welfare state strategy is more than ever likely to fail. Instead, the culture of market capitalism has to change, both in treating consumers and employees fairly, while recognising social and environmental responsibilities, and re-embedding firms within communities.

The strategy of pre-distribution will involve major changes to corporate governance discussed further below, alongside attempts to improve the bargaining power of the workforce in low-paid, insecure sectors. This will require further institutional support for unionisation, but it also involves giving individuals the resources they need to cope in different phases of working life (Ussher, 2012). This might include specific saving schemes that enable individuals to build up an asset to put towards childcare, future training needs, fulfilling caring responsibilities and undertaking voluntary service in the community matched by government support. The approach should be accompanied by a salary-insurance scheme to protect individuals against short-term setbacks and temporary unemployment. There are important proposals emerging for individual lifetime accounts that can smooth transitions such as redundancy and child rearing (Mulhern, 2013), building on the previous government's Child Trust Fund programme. This would have some of the features of a basic-income model, but it would require reciprocal responsibility on the part of the individual in making contributions, an essential feature of a more contributory welfare state.

The alternative model of progressive political economy and social reform has to address fundamental issues of economic *power*. The purpose of the pre-distribution agenda is to give individuals greater control in relation to the market, enhancing their capacity over the life-course to make meaningful choices and decisions. This reinforces the importance of rebalancing the British economy, giving individuals resources as economic agents by investing in skills, aptitudes and capabilities, increasing the capacity to bargain with powerful market actors. The importance of moving away from an agenda that reinforces the powerless passivity of individuals on an over-mighty state and big government is emphasised. This is consistent with the approach of market egalitarian thinkers such as John Rawls and James Meade. As such, the agenda represents a potent challenge to the traditional ideologies of left and right in British politics.

II. Regional banking and regional economic development

The second area for institutional reform, as part of building a new British political economy, relates to the long-term structure of financial services and the banking industry. The need to 're-balance' the British economy away from consumption and finance towards long-term investment and growth sectors such as advanced manufacturing and high-value services will only be addressed through fundamental reform of the United Kingdom banking and financial system. While access to finance is vital for any thriving market economy, the onus on encouraging and stimulating regional and local finance emphasises the importance of a more decentralised and competitive banking structure which is no longer dominated by the big five conglomerate banks.

Andrew Haldane, a senior official at the Bank of England, has pointed out that until relatively recently few would have questioned the social utility of British banks. Banks existed historically to ensure the availability of credit and loans to businesses, and to enable families to purchase homes with mortgages alongside building societies. These institutions were part of the 'social fabric' of the nation, espousing a wider notion of the public good than short-term financial gain (Haldane, 2012). Over the last 30 years, however, this role appears to have become increasingly marginalised in many banks' activities, a shift underlined by the 2008 financial crisis as the major banks were drawn into increasingly risky practices of financial intermediation.

The present government appears likely to sell-off its stake in the part-nationalised banks at the earliest opportunity, according to recent reports relating to the Royal Bank of Scotland (RBS) (Watt and Treanor, 2013). However, it would be more beneficial for the government to retain its stake in the retail banks, enforcing a clearer separation between retail and investment banking as recommended by the Vickers report and the UK Banking Commission. This would mean that the behaviour and actions of investment banks would be less likely to pose a threat to the activities of the real productive economy. The essential viability of the banking system which was imperilled in 2008 by the collapse of Lehman Brothers in the United States would no longer be at risk. There would be less need to 'bail-out' with state loans banks that took risks as part of their growth strategy; the banking system would be treated more like any other public utility which was subordinate to the needs of the economy as a whole (Gamble, 2009). Figure 3.2 shows how the largest global banks have absorbed an increasing share of banking assets, underlining the emergence of banks that are 'too big to fail'.

Figure 3.2: Share of assets as a percentage of the industry total absorbed by the five largest banks

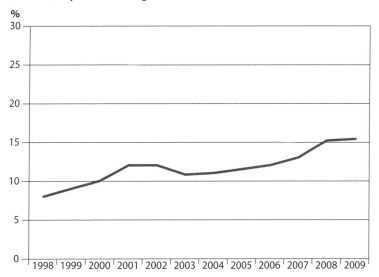

Source: 'Banking on the State' by Andrew Haldane and Piergiorgio Allessandri

Moreover, environmental scientists have drawn attention to the way in which a healthy economy, like a healthy organism, requires a *diverse ecology* in order to develop and grow sustainably. The problem of banking and finance in the UK is that the sector has become monolithic and overly centralised. Despite being at the epicentre of the capitalist system, banking has often been characterised by weak competition which leads to poorer outcomes for consumers and businesses. The purpose of regulatory intervention must be two-fold: to increase the competitiveness of the British banking system by encouraging a wider array of market entrants and a diversity of organisational forms, while creating new regional and local centres of finance which have a degree of autonomy from financial capital in the City of London. In addition, financial sector regulation has to protect the stability and resilience of the economy, ensuring that institutions do not become 'too big to fail' while passing on their externalities to the taxpayer.

Local institutions that invest locally
Both the Coalition government and the Labour opposition have advocated the creation of a national state investment bank to get more credit flowing to businesses. However, a progressive political economy ought to entail the endowment of networks of regionally-based banks which have a distinct identity and strategic role. Different regions of the UK economy have diverse needs depending on their industrial base, the skills of the workforce, requirements for SME growth, future infrastructure requirements and regionally determined priorities. The South West might focus on measures to increase the availability of finance in eco-tourism, while the North East aims to improve competitiveness and innovation in the green manufacturing sector. In particular regions, regional banks should work closely with local authorities in providing mortgages and increasing the supply of affordable housing and homes for social rent.

The Director of Civitas, David Green, argues that the Sparkassen regional banks which exist in Germany have revolutionised the system of private enterprise. The German banks improve the availability of credit to small businesses, making it less likely that loans will be withdrawn at short notice. The Sparkassen operate within the boundaries of local authorities, and cannot go beyond local districts: they currently hold one-third of business assets, and make 40 per cent of all loans to private enterprise in Germany (Green, 2012). This has enabled Germany to evolve a vibrant ecology of family-owned Mittelstand businesses, while empowering local people to solve their own problems by ensuring that bank deposits are invested in local businesses and firms. A national state investment bank with a modest capitalisation of £1 billion, together with the Regional Growth Fund of £2.4 billion as proposed by the Coalition government, will not come close to achieving this.

The opposition Labour party recently announced its conversion to the cause of regional banking (Perkins, 2013). There is a recognition that banking in the UK has become uncompetitive, given that 89 per cent of businesses depend on one of the five major high-street clearing banks. At the same time, there appears to have been a growing disconnection between the corporate strategies of the banks, focused on generating profits in the City and the property market, and the needs of customers. Duncan Wheldon from the Trade Union Congress (TUC) has shown that between 1998 and 2008, 84 per cent of the money lent by British banks was invested in property and financial services, rather than in strengthening the underlying productive capacity of the British economy (Wheldon, 2013). Since the 2008 crisis, Barclays has reduced its lending to 'non-finance, non-property-based' businesses from £52 billion to £38 billion per annum (Mason, 2012). Opposition BIS spokesperson, Toby Perkins, has revealed that Barclays has taken a further £6 billion out of manufacturing and retail businesses, putting an additional £16 billion into home loans and property (Perkins, 2013).

One of the underlying factors behind stark regional inequalities in the United Kingdom is that SME loan applications are far less likely to be successful in comparison with Britain's major economic competitors. Regions of the economy such as the North-East and North-West of England that are more dependent on SME growth are at greater risk of under-performance. It is vital to restore local relationships and trust in finance, emphasising the role of banking as a 'social utility', rather than a short-term route to profit maximisation, through a network of regional banking institutions.

A further mechanism to capitalise regional banks and provide adequate capacity is to ensure that stimulus measures such as quantitative easing (QE) operate through local banking structures, helping to improve the supply of credit flowing into financial institutions, and in turn to businesses, particularly SMEs. Only five or six per cent of bank balance sheets currently involve business lending, as banks have remained deeply conservative in their spending decisions following the financial crisis. The advantage of local institutions is that relationships of trust with local businesses and entrepreneurs enable banks to make better informed long-term investment decisions, instead of relying on corporate risk models which further restrict the supply of lending to SMEs. Again, the intangible assets of long-term trust and commitment are too often absent.

The need for an expansion of credit unions and 'peer-to-peer lending'

Credit unions are mutual financial organisations that have strong roots in local communities. In effect, credit unions are owned and managed by their members (Maer and Broughton, 2012). If the aim of economic reform is to create a more plural and competitive economy, the diversity of financial institutions operating in the United Kingdom ought to be strengthened. This can be achieved not only by creating regional and local banking institutions, but by incentivising new financial organisations such as credit unions which are adept at lending to communities with a history of financial exclusion. Indeed, credit unions and local building societies may be well suited to enabling more young people to create their own businesses, ensuring access to stable sources of long-term finance.

The expansion and penetration of credit unions in Britain has been relatively weak in comparison to the UK's international competitors. For example, in the Republic of Ireland there are 2.9 million credit union members – more than half the total population. The growth of credit unions in the United Kingdom appears to have been inhibited by legislative barriers, the regime of financial regulation which enforces prohibitive capital adequacy ratios, and the dominance of the high-street retail banks. A range of measures is being considered, both to reduce the regulatory burden and positively to encourage the expansion and growth of credit unions, especially in low-income communities. This includes the ability to pay interest rather than a dividend on deposits and to expand credit union services geographically (ABCUL, 2012).

Community Reinvestment Act to contribute a percentage of the bailout through local endowments
The concept of a Community Reinvestment Act (CRA) requires financial institutions to invest a proportion of their profits in programmes that promote improved financial outcomes for low-income areas and neighbourhoods. This might include measures to improve training and skills, and a capitalisation fund to provide finance for fledgling SMEs. The principle of the CRA is that banks should invest a defined proportion of their profits if they fail to lend and provide support to the most economically disadvantaged communities. Where there is evidence that banks are failing to ensure that financially excluded communities are adequately served, they are required to pay a financial levy as has occurred in the United States since the mid-1970s.

There has been some controversy in the United States that the CRA helped to fuel the subprime mortgage crisis by increasing the number of unsustainable home loans to low-

and middle-income households. The evidence for this is questioned, although there have been calls for much tighter regulation of mortgage lending (FRBSF, 2009). In order to inject capital into new credit unions and building societies after the crisis, all financial institutions, including retail and investment banks, should be required to contribute one per cent of the costs of the taxpayer bailout to a *financial capitalisation fund* that would encourage diversification in the financial sector, including the expansion of local banking. The German economy traditionally benefited from the culture of Mittelstand, where small and medium-sized, predominantly family-owned, businesses provide a structure for long-term lending through the Sparkassen. These strengths ought to be replicated, as far as possible, in the United Kingdom.

Rebuilding national infrastructure

A further dimension of regional economic development is strengthening public infrastructure: internal and external 'connectivity' is crucial for economic competitiveness. For instance, Parkinson *et al.* (2004) have demonstrated that the most successful cities in Europe have reliable air and rail links, underlining the importance of regional airports. Significant improvements in rail and transport infrastructure in the UK regions are urgently needed. One recent estimate suggested that 86 per cent of the government's transport infrastructure budget is currently invested in projects in London and the South East (Jacobs, 2012). In the meantime, the North East, the North West, and Yorkshire and Humberside have the highest rates of unemployment in the United Kingdom. There is the growing danger of a two-speed recovery in which London and the South pull away even further away from other UK regions (Stewart *et al.* 2013). Much greater emphasis has to be placed on strengthening the connection between regional cities as the engines of growth outside the South-East corridor.

The Armitt review is arguing for an independent national

infrastructure commission operating at arms-length from government and the civil service in Whitehall. This is similar to the persuasive case made by the London School of Economics (LSE) Growth Commission which argued that short-term political considerations too often intrude into infrastructure planning. The aim is to inject long-term horizon planning into the strategic processes that affect major decisions about infrastructure capacity, most notably in relation to aviation, high-speed rail and housing.

Another question concerns the rate of capital investment in the United Kingdom, particularly relating to investment in public sector infrastructure. Dieter Helm (2011) attests that there ought to be a clear distinction between capital and current expenditure in public accounting. Since the 2008 crisis, capital spending has been severely hit, although the current government has sought to moderate public sector spending cuts with targeted programmes of investment in public goods such as housing and the railways. It has been a recurrent feature of British recessions, nonetheless, that fiscal crises are tackled by cutting capital spending rather than current expenditure.

Much greater ambition and long-term commitment will be needed in the future. As Helm points out, borrowing to invest does not create liabilities for future generations, while borrowing for consumption creates liabilities which unfairly hit younger generations over time as debt has to be repaid. The United Kingdom needs to correct the short-term bias towards consumption which has emerged over the last 30 years, leading to unsustainable deficits, inflated asset bubbles, higher levels of household debt, inter-generational inequalities and lack of investment in capital infrastructure. There is a fundamental distinction between borrowing for consumption and borrowing for investment. Conventional economic models concentrate on GDP growth and national income, ignoring assets such as public infrastructure which are rarely included in the national accounts (Helm, 2011). This ought to be corrected by adapting conventional macro-economic and cyclical policies to foster higher levels of investment in infrastructure and public goods.

III. 'Corporate Stewardship': from shareholding to stakeholding?

The third area of institutional innovation in rebalancing the British economy relates to the constitution of the firm in the United Kingdom and the system of corporate governance. Britain has corporate governance arrangements which are still markedly 'shareholder-centric', more so than in the United States where managers have greater day-to-day autonomy and discretion (Bruner, 2011). Shareholders in the UK have more power to remove executive directors and to accept hostile takeover bids than in the United States. Nonetheless, the 2008 crisis revealed the weakness of the existing corporate governance code in preventing risk-taking activities and excessive remuneration, particularly among banks and financial institutions.

The culture of corporate governance has long been the target of reformers, going back to the 'stakeholder economy' literature of the early 1990s (Kay, 2003; Plender, 1996; Hutton, 1996).This had been fuelled in part by the behaviour of the boards of the privatised utilities during the Thatcher governments, and a series of scandals in global corporations including Enron and Parmalat. The hostile takeovers boom in the 1980s led to a number of long-standing British companies being taken over, leading to heightened public concern about the culture of mergers and acquisitions. Owen (1999) refers to the lack of involvement of institutional investors in the management of companies and the apparent ineffectiveness of company boards in challenging poor management practices. Figure 3.3 opposite illustrates the long-term trend in corporate takeovers and the cycle of M&A activity in the United Kingdom since 1969.

Figure 3.3: number of UK corporate takeovers 1969-2010

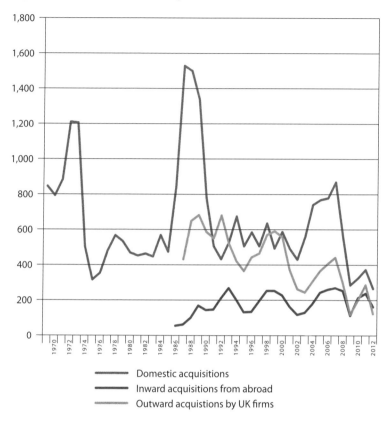

Domestic acquisitions
Inward acquisitions from abroad
Outward acquistions by UK firms

Source: ONS

The alternative stakeholder (rather than shareholder) model of the firm has several distinct advantages: one is improving the profitability and productivity of the firm through creating a culture of long-term investment; the other, more ambitiously, is embedding companies within the communities and environment they serve (Kay, 2003; Hutton, 1996). There are, of course, important distinctions between these objectives. The former emphasises the traditional virtues of the liberal market economy, stressing the importance of long-term value creation and economic efficiency. The latter stresses more communitarian goals which seek to alter the underlying structure and values of the market capitalist system.

It is important for policy-makers to be explicit about which strategic goals they are pursuing. Adair Turner (2002), for example, has argued that stakeholder models which seek to transform the values of firms within the market economy are flawed. It is important to retain the distinction between the *private realm* of market interests and the *public realm* of social interests. Companies exist to maximise value and profitability, while it is the role of the state to intervene to correct externalities and market failures. Communitarian thinkers such as Amitai Etzioni (1994) and Robert Putnum (2002) argue that no such distinction can be drawn: the priority must be to restore trust in the institutions of modern capitalism. In any society, levels of social capital will have a significant bearing on the nature and viability of competitive capitalist enterprise.

In practice, the distinction between private purposes and public virtues may have been somewhat overstated. Nevertheless, it remains important in considering institutional strategies for reform: the goal of public policy is not to force firms to behave in any particular fashion, interfering with the aims of long-term profit maximisation. Moreover, it appears unlikely that any government in Britain would seek to interfere so as explicitly to amend or redraw the corporate strategies of firms. However, it is legitimate to incentivise certain behaviours which are conducive to high-value, high-productivity and high-wage growth over the long-term.

Corporate governance reform

The United Kingdom has been subject to a series of high-level corporate governance reforms since the early 1990s (Filatotchev, Jackson, Gospel & Allcock, 2007). This includes the company law review after the Labour government's election in 1997, which revised corporate governance codes, alongside new regulations and additional legislation. According to Owen (1999), these reforms were intended to strike a more rational balance between external market pressures and internal management controls, although too little has been done to address the problems of 'passive absentee ownership' created by inactive institutional investors. Nonetheless, the post-2008 financial crisis, together with on-going concerns about short-termism in British industry and the predatory practices of institutional investors, led to renewed calls for fundamental corporate governance reform.

The Cox Review

The entrepreneur George Cox has conducted the most recent independent review of short-termism in British business (Cox, 2013). The review concludes unsurprisingly that too many firms in the United Kingdom are focused on the maximisation of returns to shareholders, rather than long-term value creation built on investment in the skills, capabilities and human capital of the workforce. Cox argues that the declining rate of investment is a major issue for the British economy, as the Asian economies have made ambitious investments in training, productivity, technology and public infrastructure over the last twenty years. The rate of investment in R&D in Britain is lower than in the United States, Japan, Germany and France. More worryingly, research-intensive sectors such as pharmaceuticals and aerospace have experienced declining research funding since the 1990s.

The Cox review accedes to the case for stronger government action. Cox draws from the analogy of the Olympics, where government investment in sport increased the United Kingdom's tally of gold medals from one at the Atlanta Olympics in 1996 to twenty nine at London 2012. It is legitimate for the state to create a long-term investment culture in the private sector. This includes proposals to encourage long-term investment in businesses: Cox proposes that capital gains tax should be tapered on shares from 50 per cent in year one of ownership to 10 per cent after ten years to incentivise long-term shareholding. Companies should be encouraged to issue different classifications of shares, with committed shareholders attracting preferential dividends or bonus shares; shares held for significant periods may be subject to a beneficial tax regime.

More radically, Cox argues that investment and pension funds should be taxed on the incomes they generate just as individuals are taxed currently. He proposes that 30 per cent of executive remuneration could be deferred for up to five years, so pay better reflects long-term performance. As in the Kay review, Cox insists that quarterly reporting should be phased out since it further encourages short-termism. In relation to takeovers, shareholders appearing on the share register during the offer period should be excluded from voting until a bid has been concluded.

Both the Cox and Kay reviews agree that there needs to be greater scope to take account of the national interest in takeover decisions, which the previous government was unable to do, most notably in relation to the Kraft Foods takeover of Cadbury. This was a disquieting event for ministers not least because Cadbury was an apparently well-run company which had outperformed Kraft, and which had strong local roots and a sense of local identity. Roger Carr, then Chairman of Cadbury, observed that: 'individuals controlling shares which they had owned for only a few days or weeks determined the destiny of a company that had been built over almost 200 years' (Peston, 2010). Raising the threshold for a takeover from 50 to 60 per cent while ensuring that those who vote owned the shares for at least a year would have enabled the Cadbury board to see off a hostile bid (Bailey, 2012). Indeed, it is more important than ever to protect the principle of stewardship, enhancing the long-term value of British businesses.

Widening employee share ownership

Another strategy to change the culture of firms is to widen the base of employee share ownership. The Thatcher government introduced employee share ownership plans (ESOP) in the mid-1980s to accompany the sale of national utilities, but the shares were soon bought up in corporate takeovers, and the level of employee share ownership declined significantly. It ought to be made easier for businesses to give their workers an equity stake in firms, and this should be augmented by profit-sharing schemes. Share ownership should be more actively encouraged among employees, and to this end the Cox review proposes that workers should have the right to be paid up to five per cent of their basic salary in shares, to a maximum of £5,000 per annum.

The 'S-Corporation' in the United States

A further approach to corporate governance reform is the model of the 'S-corporation' in the United States which has grown from 2.7 to 4.5 million firms over the last ten years. The S-Corporation uses tax incentives to encourage long-term value creation alongside growth in family-owned businesses and SMEs. The aim is to ensure the company does not pay tax on capital gains if the profits are reinvested in productive assets, an alternative to the traditional British model of the plc. The aim is to advance a custodian model of the firm by limiting the number and classification of shareholders. This means that S-corporations in the United States are effectively exempt from corporation tax. Their ability to generate investment internally means they are less reliant on finance through the banks (Green, 2012).

The Company Law Review in the late 1990s made important proposals for reform which, unfortunately, were not taken up by the previous government. The current leadership of the Labour Party is aiming to enforce a distinction between 'predators' and 'producers' in the British economy, emphasising the importance of sustainable value creation. However, the question remains as to whether legislative changes are too blunt an instrument in comparison with tax incentives and other forms of regulatory intervention. Similarly, Mayer (2012) emphasised the fundamental importance of shareholders fulfilling their legal responsibilities in embedding a culture of corporate stewardship in the UK economy.

IV. The civic economy: pluralisation and new approaches to ownership

The final pillar of an active, state-led institutional strategy concerns the development of a genuinely bottom-up, localised economy promoting greater pluralism in the structures of ownership, the constitution of the firm and the nature of economic activity. According to the National Endowment for Science, Technology and the Arts (NESTA), the notion of the *civic economy* is distinctive (NESTA, 2011). First, it aims to integrate social and economic outcomes, combining financial gain with social impact. This is not a rejection of the profit motive, but an attempt to rebuild trust in institutions and to promote integrity in market transactions. Moreover, the civic economy is capable of bridging the local and the global through networks of social and human capital, aided by the application of ICT and new technologies. Finally, the civic economy aims to mobilise existing assets rather than passively meeting consumer needs, drawing on the capabilities and strengths of the local population.

Michael Sandel's recent book *How Markets Crowd Out Morals* (2012) implicitly develops the rationale for the civic economy, arguing that markets have a tendency to crowd out and displace civic virtue. The shift towards the civic economy may be compatible with prospective patterns of structural change in the British economy, however, characterised by Murray (2009) as the emergence of a 'third frontier' *associative economy* replacing the Fordist system of mass production. While structural changes in recent decades have focused on the shift from manufacturing industry to various service-orientated sectors, there are likely to be additional changes in the nature of the service-based economy in the coming years. The most salient are:

◆ That the *consumers and users of services are more implicated than ever in their production and design* – captured in the notion of the 'prosumer'. Most modern companies use intelligence and insight from their own customers in order to evolve the next generation of products and services.

◆ Second, *social pressures are creating new patterns of demand for services*, particularly in the public sector: ageing, demographic change, the growth of obesity and chronic diseases. These are further demands that traditional services are often poorly equipped to meet, while reducing costs and improving productivity has proved almost impossible within traditional delivery systems. The civic economy also challenges the dichotomy between states and markets, alongside the implicit division between the public and private sectors.

The associative economy emphasises the importance of collaboration, trust and reciprocity, a useful corrective in the aftermath of the financial crisis. Moreover, the incentivisation of pluralised structures of activity and ownership is a vital instrument in economic *rebalancing*. Mayer (2012) argues powerfully in favour of corporate pluralism, since different types of company have particular strategic strengths: the classic Anglo-American firm is able to take rapid and decisive decisions about job-shedding and cost reduction. German companies, on the other hand, focus on long-term investment, sustaining the commitment of the workforce through a culture of social partnership. The British economy needs a diverse ecosystem of organisations and firms. Arguably, an unbalanced economy is characterised by too many monopolies and oligopolies in product, labour and capital markets. For example, prior to the 2008 financial crisis, more than 90 per cent of lending to firms occurred through one of five dominant high-street banks. Intriguingly, mortgage lending by building societies has risen substantially since January 2012.

However, the ownership structures of the British economy have remained largely monolithic. In relation to the constitution of firms, examples of employee-owned businesses and trusts such as the John Lewis Partnership stand out since they are so unusual in the United Kingdom. Moreover, the British economy remains highly geared towards finance. In the 1980s and 1990s, deindustrialisation was positively promoted by British governments through maintaining an artificially high exchange rate, leading to the decline of manufacturing industry in comparison to finance.

Figure 3.4: Gross lending by British Building Societies

£000,000

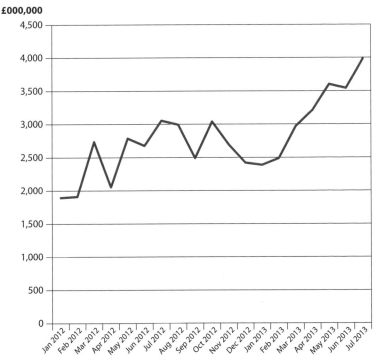

Source: Building Societies Association

But pluralisation is a challenge as much for the Left as for the Right in British politics. Tristram Hunt (2011) insists that the Labour party had become too dependent on the state as the primary mechanism of resisting the outcomes produced by the market. The British centre-left had abandoned its associational heritage, the legacy of co-ops, mutual societies and trade unions whose original mission had been actively to redistribute economic power. The aim of public policy should be to encourage new forms of association that protect those in the middle and lower end of the income distribution, rather than relying on state intervention to promote fairness.

In 2010, *The Economist* argued: 'Just as an ecosystem benefits from diversity, so the world is better off with a multitude of corporate forms'.[7] The lesson of the period since the crisis is that pluralisation does not occur spontaneously but requires active government intervention and regulatory action. Otherwise, existing models of financialised, shareholder capitalism are allowed to become too dominant. The weakness of the United Kingdom policy framework has been a tendency to implement generic, horizontal pro-enterprise policy. Instead, more vertical sector-specific policies are required to promote the high-tech manufacturing sector through targeted corporation tax concessions, alongside employment incentives via the National Insurance system.

The focus on sectors should help to create more high-value, well-paid jobs. Between 1979 and 2009, manufacturing employment in the UK shrank from seven million to 2.5 million, yet manufacturing employment is generally more secure and well paid than services (Sperling, 2005). As a consequence, former industrial areas in the North of England have experienced a long-term unemployment rate of at least 20 per cent. In reality, more than half the new jobs created under the 1997-2010 Labour government were publicly funded, which meant that regional economic development was rarely self-sustaining (Cobham *et al.*, 2013). Instead,

---

7 Cited in Michie (2010).

public policy approaches are required where government spending is focused on 'transitional investment' in sectors such as digital, energy, transport, and infrastructure: future-orientated sectors where public investment does not seek artificially to preserve old technologies and service models (Murray, 2009).

Procurement

One additional area for public policy intervention is procurement to extend and diversify the supply-chain in key sectors, giving more opportunities to fledgling businesses and SMEs. The UK government currently spends £227 billion on purchasing goods and services through the public sector. More support is, in turn, required for local, home-grown businesses through the management of the procurement supply chain. There are instances where procurement can be used to promote manufacturing industry: for example in the case of Bombardier, a British-based company producing rolling-stock for the train network, the government initially refused to intervene to ensure a key contract went to a domestic company for fear of contravening European Union State Aid rules (Gribben, 2011). Most EU member states already use procurement to favour national businesses, however. Procurement strategies should not prevent ministers from championing national enterprises. It is vital that national and regional supply-chains are re-established, particularly in sectors such as the automotive industry. There is a case for using associated levers of procurement to support research-intensive businesses, a further catalyst towards innovation and growth.

Promoting SMEs

The recent report by Lord Young emphasised the importance of small and medium-sized enterprises in the British economy, with greater numbers than ever seeking to create their own businesses (Young, 2013). SMEs comprise 99 per cent of all businesses in the UK, employing 14.1 million people and constituting more than 60 per cent of private sector employment. SMEs have grown from less than one million in the early 1970s to nearly five million today. Moreover, seven per cent of SMEs create half of all jobs in the UK economy. According to the Small Business Taskforce, nine out of ten unemployed people have found work in an SME since 2008. The expansion of 'micro-businesses' appears to have accelerated even further since the crisis.

SMEs generate significant social and economic benefits. They increasingly challenge the way in which large incumbent corporations operate through applying innovation, while using R&D to create new products and services in sectors from software design and video-gaming to bio-engineering. Moreover, small businesses are important in ensuring that wealth generated locally remains in that particular geographic area (Lent *et al.*, 2013). For instance, according to research recently carried out by the New Economics Foundation (NEF), every £10 spent on local, organic groceries was worth £25 for the local area, compared with £14 when the same amount was spent in a national supermarket chain (2002).

Nonetheless, the growth of SMEs has been curtailed by the inadequacy of bank finance and lending through local institutions. In recent years, governments have recognised the importance of encouraging innovation and entrepreneurship in the small business sector, particularly in the creative and software industries, as well as less knowledge-intensive sectors such as social care. This includes not only for-profit companies, but also mutual businesses, social enterprises, SMEs and co-operatives. Gamble (2009) emphasises that a progressive political economy requires a vibrant and diverse ecology of enterprises and firms. National governments have powerful levers to promote this sustainable ecology, since the Treasury controls over eighty per cent of the R&D budget through tax credits which are used to support small business innovation.

Sainsbury (2013) shows how, in the United States, the

federal government effectively targets resources on scientific and technological research. Despite being a liberal market economy analogous to the United Kingdom, government agencies are engaged in identifying important technological breakthroughs in sectors such as computing and genetic engineering (Mazzucato, 2011). In the last 45 years, 58 out of the 100 most innovative commercial products in the United States were created through federal government-funded laboratories, universities and public agencies. Seventy-five per cent of innovations approved by the Food and Drug Administration in the United States between 1993 and 2004 owe their discovery to initial public investment through the National Institute of Health (Mazzucato, 2013). The funding which supported Apple in its early phase came from government-backed small business innovation programmes. Professor David Bailey has referred to the role of the Small Business Administration (SBA) in the United States, which acts in effect as a state investment bank. This supports SMEs struggling to gain support through the banking and financial system, alongside a generous infrastructure of R&D tax credits and capital allowances. The US operates a 'shadow' developmental state where barriers to innovation such as high costs, uncertainty and information asymmetries are addressed through consistent state support (Mazzucato, 2013).

The nature of the markets in which SMEs compete is changing rapidly. Recent estimates suggested that 75 per cent of global growth will occur in emerging market economies, with an additional $30 trillion of demand from the new global middle class which is rapidly emerging. Today, 30 per cent of manufacturing exports are from developing states; in the early 1980s, it was less than ten per cent (Sainsbury, 2013), indicating a fundamental shift in the nature of global production.

Some commentators refer to this as a more fundamental shift than the industrial revolution – from globalisation to worldwide 'economic democratisation'. This emphasises that the structural processes unfolding are moving away from mass markets towards smaller niche markets. If the purpose of government intervention in the 1960s and 1970s was to prop up ailing industries and large-scale enterprises, protecting firms that faced a major threat from international competitors, the goal today is to support economic growth in strategic sectors, much of it driven by micro-businesses and small business entrepreneurs.

Lent, Painter and Sen (2013) refer to the importance of challenging concentrations of power that predominate, limiting the potential of producers, inventors, wealth-creators and innovators. This can be as important in advancing fairness and social justice as conventional income transfers through the welfare state. At present, the policy, legal and legislative framework in the United Kingdom is still heavily biased in favour of corporate big business, in everything from regulatory action and procurement to planning law and patent restrictions. This reinforces monopolies and oligopolies which have predominated in the United Kingdom economy since the Second World War. Reinventing the spirit of entrepreneurship and small business creation in Britain will not only create wealth: it will help to ensure that wealth is more evenly distributed and dispersed throughout the economy.

Forging an innovation-driven economy
The importance of SMEs relates to the centrality of *innovation* in increasing the underlying productive potential of the economy. There are four key aspects of an innovation eco-system: funding research; promoting knowledge transfer; using demand to stimulate innovation; and managing the transition from innovation into commercially marketable products and services. Despite efforts by the previous administration to invest significantly in science, duly maintained by the current Coalition government, R&D spending in the British economy has remained significantly below that of France, Germany and Sweden, as Figure 3.5

illustrates below. This, in part, reflects the fact that R&D-intensive sectors account for a smaller share of GDP in Britain compared with countries such as Germany.

Figure 3.5: 2011 R&D spending as a percentage of GDP by country

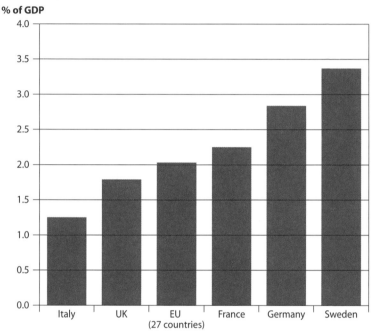

Source: ONS

There is a traditional distinction between basic academic and applied research; the United Kingdom has traditionally been strong on basic research, ranking third in the world for cited publications after the United States and China, while British universities are generally highly regarded. Of the top fifty universities in the world, eleven are in Europe, of which five are located in the United Kingdom. Higher education institutions remain a major economic asset for Britain. However, what the United Kingdom appears to have lacked historically is strong links between research institutions and the commercial sector: higher education has been relatively weak at knowledge-transfer, although the share of private investment in universities has increased markedly since the 1990s (Sainsbury, 2013).

Government has to make use of all of the levers at its disposal: for example, the NHS procurement budget can make a significant impact on innovation within the pharmaceuticals sector. There have already been attempts to replicate the Franzhofer Institutes in Germany which, drawing on government support, translate higher education research into marketable commercial products. The digital revolution in the United States was actively promoted by the state through the provision of technological infrastructure, guaranteeing intellectual property rights. Markets always require underpinning through rules overseen by governments if they are to develop and operate effectively.

Regional Development Agencies and Local Economic Partnerships
Diversifying Britain's economic base and sowing the seeds of a revitalised civil economy strongly implies that the strategy of regional banking and lending ought to be complemented by the strengthening of regional economic institutions. Figureheads are required to promote and drive inward investment in regional infrastructure projects and businesses. At present, there is a risk that infrastructure policies will merely exacerbate regional inequalities: 84 per cent of infrastructure spending goes to London and the South East. The proposed high-speed (HS2) rail-line would act as a spur to job creation and growth, but there are too few local spin-offs that benefit the North East and North West of England. Regional institutions are better placed to decide where public investment ought to be used effectively, in particular by helping to promote 'clusters'. The former RDAs have played a crucial role in anticipating shocks and diversifying the supply chain, such as in the West Midlands following the closure of MG Rover in the mid-2000s (Bailey, 2012). The role of active industrial policy is, in part, to help different companies and sectors to understand how

the shape of markets is changing so that they can plan and prepare strategically for change (Rodrik, 2008).

Building local economies from the bottom-up

As importantly, local authorities should have greater freedom and capacity to tax, raise precepts and borrow in order to invest in local public infrastructure and public goods. There ought to be a general presumption of competence; financing should be achieved through programmes such as bond issuance against local authority pension funds, given that local government pension fund assets amount to more than £161 billion. This would help to improve the ability of local councils to address the dire shortage of affordable and socially rented housing. However, the role of local councils is not simply to spend resources and provide services: local government is also a crucial engine of economic growth.

The decentralisation of power means giving local political actors additional scope to provide strategic leadership; businesses need a single point of contact in local areas where they can get advice and support to incentivise long-term investment decisions. While there are criticisms of the mayoral model in England, there are few other obvious routes to providing clear political leadership; mayors of city-regions can bring together services and infrastructure on a far larger scale, as is occurring in the North East where seven local authorities in Tyneside and Teeside are pooling their resources to create a joint authority overseeing the wider region. Parkinson *et al.* (2004) show that cities in continental Europe are able to raise more revenue locally: they are less dependent on the central state and able to pursue long-term strategies. Cities are generally more pro-active, entrepreneurial and competitive: the lesson is that 'letting go' can have a decisive impact on economic success.

Local councils oversee significant local supply chains through public procurement, tendering and contracting-out. In the past, contracts have more often been awarded to the largest firms who have the advantage of scale; however, it is vital to enable SMEs to compete on a level playing field, particularly in areas where they might employ a higher proportion of workers from black and minority ethnic backgrounds. Another area where local councils possess significant levers is regeneration policy: partnerships between the public and private sectors can be an important driver of growth and employment in neighbourhoods that have suffered historically high levels of economic exclusion and worklessness.

The creative economy

According to NESTA, the creative economy accounts for around ten per cent of output in the British economy, providing 2.5 million jobs – more than financial services or advanced manufacturing. Employment growth in creative sectors is four times greater than for the economy as a whole, and Britain is genuinely world-leading in the creative sector (Bakhshi, Hargreaves & Mateos-Garcia, 2013). Moreover, the creative industries are forecast to grow at twice the rate of the economy, and the UK has among the largest advertising, music and video game markets in the world (CBI, 2011).

Nonetheless, policy-makers in the United Kingdom have not kept pace with other countries over the last fifteen years. It is vital that the Internet remains as open as possible, while tax relief and procurement rules have to maximise the potential for innovation. Moreover, public institutions from the BBC to universities have to maximise their contribution to the digital economy, and investment in broadband ought to be a key component of the British government's plans for capital investment in public infrastructure. At the same time, 'soft' infrastructure such as the quality of the local environment, culture, the arts, creative sectors and architecture are often key to attracting and retaining talent in city-regions – a key motor of long-term growth.

Manufacturing matters

Finally, a strategy for the pluralisation and diversification of the British economy means that additional measures are needed to promote UK manufacturing industry. There is a need for greater exchange rate stability in order to assist manufacturing; otherwise, firms will never invest in plant, machinery and new technologies. By 2009, the UK had a goods deficit on the current account of £90 billion. There has been a rapid and steady decline in manufacturing investment since the 1980s. There is a strong case for capital allowances in manufacturing, alongside R&D tax credits. Indeed, the British government recently reduced capital allowances which firms use to pay for plant and equipment in order to fund a corporation tax cut: for many the wrong strategic priority.

Professsor David Bailey from Coventry University has focused on the importance of active industrial policy in managing supply chains. He cites the example of Vauxhall at Ellesmere Port where only 25 per cent of the vehicle components are actually made in the United Kingdom. The content of a JCB digger manufactured in the domestic market has declined from 96 per cent in the late 1970s to less than 40 per cent today. Focusing on manufacturing sector growth *per se* will merely suck more component imports into the British economy: overseeing the supply chain means supporting SMEs to win contracts from larger firms so that the extent of beneficial spill-overs into the United Kingdom are maximised.

There are other measures through which governments might use the tax system more effectively (Bailey, 2012). For example, firms which deliver improvements in export performance in the manufacturing sector, or who take on younger workers and increase the supply of apprenticeships, should be awarded national insurance holidays. Despite the strategic importance of manufacturing as a source of relatively secure, well-paid jobs and faster GDP growth, it is important not to neglect unfashionable sectors in measures to strengthen productivity, notably food processing, alongside services such as health, social care and education. Many of the jobs of the future will be located in those sectors: the United Kingdom has significant comparative advantage and strengths on which it ought to build.

While sceptics have questioned the feasibility of a renaissance in traditional British manufacturing industry, it certainly appears realistic for the UK share of hi-tech manufacturing to converge with that of states such as Germany and Finland; this would require little more than recapturing the pre-2000 levels of growth in those sectors (Oxford Economics, 2010). The evidence indicates that high-tech manufacturing sectors are particularly responsive to increased innovation activity, alongside higher rates of spending on research and development (R&D). There is the opportunity to build on existing strengths and sources of comparative advantage in sectors such as aerospace and civil aviation, printing and publishing, and the food and beverage sectors. This will create the conditions for faster growth both in high-value manufacturing and knowledge-intensive service industries.

4

Conclusion

This book has focused on the long-term prospects for the British economy, alongside the institutional configuration of political economy and its historical development in the post-war period. A crucial issue not so far addressed is the international and global dimension of economic reform. Whatever institutional changes are carried out in the British economy, the system of European and global economic governance will continue to have a crucial bearing on economic outcomes in a domestic context. Since the Second World War, Britain has been part of a liberal economic order predicated on open immigration policies, free trade, integration into the European Union, and strong ties to the North Atlantic free trade area (Gamble, 2009). There have been setbacks and reversals, not least Britain's 'awkward partner' status in Europe since the 1950s. But this has been the underlying trajectory of British policy upheld by all the major parties.

There is growing evidence that the dominant consensus may be under challenge, given the apparent growth of protectionist, nationalist and xenophobic pressures in British politics as symbolised by growing support for the UK Independence Party (UKIP). These are not inexorable forces but they are an expression of deep, underlying discontentment and frustration at the paucity of the alternatives offered by the current political establishment. The argument of this book is that measures to strengthen national policies and national strategies are not antithetical to ensuring constructive regulation and oversight of the international economy through the World Bank, the International Monetary Fund, the International Labour Organisation (ILO), the G20 and the European Union. The need for closer international co-operation is stronger than ever: in relation to the future of the United Kingdom's EU membership, it should be remembered that Britain still exports more goods and services to Belgium and Luxembourg than it does to China. Leaving the EU single market would pose a significant threat to long-term British prosperity.

The capabilities of the state

It is clear that an activist policy regime designed to rebalance the British economy needs strong and effective political and economic institutions. This book has argued that *active government* has a crucial role to play as the *enabler, innovator, regulator* and *equaliser* in a more balanced and cohesive economy. A succession of reviews on the UK growth challenge have alluded to the importance of 'good governance'. The World Bank has confirmed through comparative surveys that the quality of government and the efficiency of the public sector are crucial for a country's growth prospects. While government's role and the importance of active industrial policy has too easily been undermined by the implicit shift towards neo-liberal policies in the last thirty years, the quality of policy-making and implementation within the UK state has often been inadequate.

It is apparent that the crisis will not herald a major expansion in the political and economic frontiers of the state, as some on the left would dearly wish to see. This is a question of the *effectiveness* of the state, rather than the *size* of the state: a large state measured as a percentage of GDP, or by the size of public sector employment, need be no more effective in dealing robustly with the externalities created by neo-liberalism. It is not the nominal size of government that matters, but its efficacy.

Moreover, policy-making structures in Whitehall have historically been characterised by an 'amateurish' approach, relying on too little specialist knowledge, detailed comparative analysis, benchmarking and systematic review of the evidence to inform policy-making. At the same time, the fragmentation of the state into a series of agencies and non-departmental public bodies has confused accountabilities, making it harder to discern who is responsible for what in British government. Clarifying the nature of ministerial and departmental responsibility will be necessary to implement the wider reforms addressed in this book.

This relates specifically to the role of the Department for Business, Industry and Skills (BIS), which has historically occupied a weak position within the Whitehall hierarchy, given the institutional strength of the Treasury. A previous Labour Prime Minister, Harold Wilson, sought to combat the Treasury's power by creating the Department of Economic Affairs (DEA) and the Ministry of Technology in 1964, envisaging a stronger voice for industry in Whitehall as part of the modernising 'white heat of technological revolution'. The DEA was tasked with delivering the 'National Plan' and its nominal growth target for the British economy of four per cent per annum. Although the DEA struggled to have an impact against the backdrop of successive balance of payment crises and 'stop-go' economic policy, and was subsequently abolished in 1970, a key question remains about the extent of departmental capacity in Whitehall to forge an active industrial policy.

As a department, BIS needs more stable leadership, with officials who have sector-specific expertise, boosted by private sector secondments, as would be taken for granted in the French state, alongside stronger local roots in the cities and regions of the UK economy (Adonis, 2013). There is a strong case for creating an economics 'super-ministry' incorporating the Department for Business, Innovation and Skills (BIS), the Department for Communities and Local

Government (DCLG), and the productivity functions of the Treasury (HMT). This would provide a real locus for economic and political decentralisation, alongside stable relationships of trust and commitment between the public and private sectors which Britain lacked throughout much of the post-war period.

Reconciling the political and the moral economy

A more fundamental question underlying the need for an institutional strategy to rebalance the British economy is the importance of reconciling the political with the moral economy (Gamble, 2012). Many of the issues discussed in this book concern technocratic questions of economic efficiency, technology, human capital, productivity, industrial policy, alongside the relative role and size of the state. But the financial crisis has underlined the importance of the 'moral' economy: how far dominant patterns of economic production and exchange are compatible with underlying human values and sentiments, alongside the sustainability and cohesion of society. The goal of policy must be to bring together the values of the *moral* and *political* economy, expressing an ethical as well as a technocratic vision of a 'good economy'.

This emphasises that the tradition of writing about political economy since Adam Smith has been deeply concerned with how economies reinforce and uphold notions of the public interest. In *The Moral Consequences of Economic Growth*, Benjamin Friedman (2006) attests that societies with stable levels of growth and rising living standards are more likely to be successful, open, tolerant, dynamic and future-orientated. Capitalism is created by human endeavour, not invisible forces, and the institutions that oversee the capitalist economy have constantly to be reformed and adapted to be effective and to meet wider human needs and purposes.

Capitalism has fundamental weaknesses, as Adair Turner (2002) has described. The capitalist system does not produce an acceptable distribution of outcome and opportunity; nor do free markets create an adequate supply of collective public goods; product, capital and labour markets are imperfect and can fail, occasionally with catastrophic consequences; and there are always incentives that ought to be advanced beyond self-interest and rational market exchange. For much of the last two decades, Whitehall and Westminster have been prone to uncritical 'pro-market' thinking, including now seemingly erroneous confidence in the self-regulating capacities of financial markets (Cobham *et al.*, 2013).

Of course, all governments need to demonstrate that they can govern the economy competently. But they also need a wider economic and political narrative which can shape events – not just passively respond to them. Political leaders need to develop a vision of the type of economy and society that Britain should aspire to be. It is therefore imperative that capitalism is moderated and overseen by accountable and effective public institutions. The role of government should be to identify credible interventions that improve the supply of collective goods and enhance the effectiveness of regulatory regimes, without undermining the dynamic forces of markets. In the twenty-first century, Britain needs an approach which restores the role of public institutions in forging an economy where social justice, personal liberty, economic growth and ecological sustainability are judiciously combined.

Bibliography

A. Adonis, 'A smarter BIS: A review of the Department of Business, Science and Innovation', 10 July 2013, London: Policy Network/IPPR.

K. Aiginger, 'Industrial Policy: A Dying Bird or a Re-emerging Phoenix?', *Journal of Competitive Trade*, 7, 2007, pp. 297-323.

Association of British Credit Unions Limited, 'Credit unions set to expand and take on banks', 8 January 2012, [online], available at: http://www.which.co.uk/news/2012/01/credit-unions-set-to-expand-and-take-on-banks-275820/ [Accessed 02/09/2013].

H. Bakhshi, I. Hargreaves & J. Mateos-Garcia, *A Manifesto for the Creative Economy*, London: NESTA, 2013.

D. Bailey, 'Strategies for Rebalancing', in T. Hunt (ed.), *Rebalancing the British Economy*, London: Civitas, 2012.

C.M. Bruner, 'Corporate Governance Reform in a Time of Crisis', *The Journal of Corporation Law*, Volume 36 (2), June 2011.

D. Cobham, C. Adam & K. Mayhew, 'The Economic Record of the 1997-2010 Labour government: an assessment', *Oxford Review of Economic Policy*, 29, 2013, pp. 47-70.

Commons Library Standard Note on Credit Unions, 16 November 2011, [online], available at: http://www.parliament.uk/briefing-papers/SN01034 [Accessed 02/09/2013].

Confederation of British Industry (CBI), 'A vision for rebalancing the economy: a new approach to growth', December 2011.

K. Coutts & R. Rowthorn, 'Prospects for the UK Balance of Payments', *Cambridge Centre for Business Research Working Paper* No. 394, 2009.

G. Cox, 'Overcoming Short-termism within British Business', Labour Party Report, February 2013, [online], available at: http://www.yourbritain.org.uk/uploads/editor/files/Overcoming_Short-termism.pdf [Accessed 02/09/2013].

N. Crafts, 'British Economic Decline Revisited', *University of Warwick Working Paper Series*, 42, May 2011.

C.A.R. Crosland, *The Future of Socialism*, London: Robinson Publishing, 1956.

C. Crouch, *The Strange Non-Death of Neo-Liberalism*, Cambridge: Polity, 2010.

G. Davies, 'A case for cautious optimism on the British economy', *The Financial Times*, 5 September 2013.

A. Daripa, S. Kapur & S. Wright, 'Labour's Record on Financial Regulation', *Oxford Review of Economic Policy*, 29 (1), 2013, pp.71-94.

Department of Business, Innovation and Skills, 'A Strategy for Sustainable Growth', London: HMG, 1 July 2010.

A. De Waal, 'Education in England: Policy *vs.* Impact', London: Civitas, 2009.

A. Etzioni, *The Spirit of Community: The Reinvention of American Society*, New York: Touchstone, 1994.

European Commission, 'Teaching and Learning: Towards the Learning Society', EU Commission White Paper, 1995.

Federal Reserve Bank of San Francisco, 'Perspectives on the Future of the Community Reinvestment Act', February 2009, [online], available at: www.frbsf.org/community-development/publications/community-development-investment-review/2009/february/future-cra-community-reinvestment-act/ [Accessed 02/09/2013].

A. Filatotchev, I. Jackson, S. Gospel & S. Allcock, 'Identifying the key drivers of "good" corporate governance and the appropriateness of policy responses', *DTI Economics Paper*, 2007, pp. 1-227.

B. Friedman, *The Moral Consequences of Economic Growth*, London: Vintage, 2006.

J. Froud *et al.* 'Must the ex-industrial regions fail?', *Soundings*, 2013.

A. Gamble, 'Debt and Deficits: The Quest for Economic Competence', in O. Cramme & P. Diamond, *After the Third Way: The Future of the Left in Europe*, London: IB Tauris, 2012.

A. Gamble, 'Economic Futures', *The British Academy New Paradigms in Public Policy Series*, 2011.

A. Gamble, *The Spectre at the Feast: Capitalist Crisis and the Politics of Recession*, Basingstoke: Palgrave Macmillan, 2009.

D. Green, 'Regional Banks' in T. Hunt (ed.), *Rebalancing the British Economy*, London: Civitas, 2012.

R. Gribben, 'Bombardier plant in Derby could be saved by state train aid', *The Telegraph*, 4 December 2011.

J. Hacker, 'The Institutional Foundations of Middle-Class Democracy', *Policy Network*, 6 May 2011.

A. Haldane, 'A Leaf Being Turned', speech to Occupy Economics 'Socially Useful' Banking Conference, 29 October 2012.

P. Hall & D. Soskice, *Varieties of Capitalism: The Institutional Foundations of Comparative Advantage*, Oxford: Oxford University Press, 2001.

C. Hay, 'The Strange Demise of the Anglo-Liberal Growth Model', *2010 Leonard Schapiro Lecture*, University of Princeton, 2010.

D. Helm, 'Public Assets', Social Market Foundation, November 2011.

T. Hunt, 'Reviving Our Sense of Mission: Designing a New Political Economy', in R. Philpott (ed.), *The Purple Book*, London: Biteback, 2011.

W. Hutton, *The State We're In*, London: Vintage, 1996.

Institute for Fiscal Studies, 'Living Standards, Poverty and Inequality in the UK: 2013', June 2013.

E. Jacobs, 'Rail investments need to be the start of something bigger', *The Guardian*, 20 July 2012.

A. Kaletsky, 'The City got its way but might just regret it', *The Times*, 19 May 2010.

J. Kay, *The Truth About Markets*, London: Penguin, 2003.

G. Kelly, 'Why the Squeezed Middle is here to stay', *The Guardian*, 21 May 2012.

J.M. Keynes, *The General Theory of Employment, Interest and Money*, London: Macmillan, 1935.

P. Krugman, *Depression Economics and the Crisis of 2008*, New York: Vintage, 2009.

Labour Policy Review, 'Skills Taskforce Interim Report: Talent Matters – why England needs a new approach to skills', 21 May 2013, [online] available at: http://www.yourbritain.org.uk/uploads/editor/files/170513_Talent_matters_Policy_Review.pdf [Accessed 02/09/2013].

S. Lansley, *The Cost of Inequality: Why Economic Equality is Essential for Recovery*, London: Gibson Square, 2011.

S. Lansley & H. Reed, 'How to Increase the Wage Share', *TUC Touchstone Pamphlet*, June 2013.

J. Le Grand, *Motivation, Agency and Public Policy*, Oxford: Oxford University Press, 2007.

A. Lent, A. Painter & H. Sen, 'Moving Labour "into the Black"', Policy Network, 19 June 2013.

LSE Growth Commission report, 'Investing for Prosperity: Skills, Infrastructure and Innovation', London: London School of Economics, 2012.

R. Lupton, 'Labour's Social Policy Record: Spending and Outcomes 1997-2010', STICERD, London School of Economics, July 2013.

McKinsey Global Institute, 'Education to Employment: Designing a system that works', January 2013.

L. Maer and N. Broughton, 'Financial Services: contribution to the UK economy', SN/EP/06193, London: House of Commons Library, 21 August 2012.

D. Marquand, *The Unprincipled Society*, London: Fontana, 1989.

P. Mason, 'Behold, the British establishment, panicked', BBC online, 3 July 2012, available at: http://www.bbc.co.uk/news/business-18688417 [Accessed 02/09/2013].

C. Mayer, *Firm Commitment: Why the corporation is failing us*, Oxford: Oxford University Press, 2012.

M. Mazzucato, *The Entrepreneurial State*, London: Demos, 2011.

M. Mazzucato, *The Entrepreneurial State: Debunking Public vs. Private Sector Myths*, London: Anthem Books, 2013.

J. Meadway *et al.*, 'The Good Jobs Plan', New Economics Foundation, 31 March 2011.

J. Michie, 'Promoting corporate diversity in the financial services sector', 9 September 2010, [online], available at: http://www. kellogg.ox.ac.uk/sites/kellogg/files/documents/Corporate_Diversity_Report.pdf [Accessed: 02/09/2013]

J. Mills, *An Exchange Rate Target: Why we need one*, Civitas, April 2013.

Morgan Stanley Research, Global Outlook report, 28 November 2011, p.26.

I. Mulhern, 'Does Labour have the political will to introduce contributory welfare?', *The Guardian*, 27 May 2013.

R. Murray, 'Danger and Opportunity: Crisis and the new social economy', NESTA, 17 September 2009.

National Endowment for Science, Technology and the Arts (NESTA), 'Rebalancing Act: research report', June 2010.

NESTA, *Compendium for a Civic Economy*, May 2011, [online], available at: http://www.nesta.org.uk/assets/features/compendium_for_the_civic_economy [Accessed 02/09/2013].

New Economics Foundation, 'Plugging the leaks: Making the most of every pound that enters your local economy', September 2002, [online], available at: http://www.pluggingtheleaks.org/downloads/ptl_handbook.pdf [Accessed 02/09/2013].

J. Norman & J. Ganesh, 'Compassionate Conservatism', Policy Exchange, 13 September 2006.

Office for Budget Responsibility (OBR), Economic and fiscal outlook, March 2013, [online], available at: http://cdn.budgetresponsibility.independent.gov.uk/March-2013-EFO-44734674673453.pdf [Accessed 02/09/2013].

G. Owen, *The rise and fall of great companies: Courtaulds and the reshaping of the man-made fibres industry*, Oxford: Oxford University Press, 2010.

G. Owen, *From empire to Europe: the decline and revival of British industry since the Second World War*, London: Harper Collins, 1999.

Oxford Economics, 'Examining Sectoral Growth in the UK', a report for NESTA, June 2010.

A. Painter, *Left Without a Future? Social Justice in Anxious Times*, London: Policy Network, 2013.

M. Parkinson *et al.*, 'Competitive European Cities: Where do the core cities stand?', report to the Office of the Deputy Prime Minister (ODPM), January 2004.

C. Peretz, *Technological Revolutions and Financial Capital: The Dynamics of Bubbles and Golden Ages,* Edward Elgar Publishing, 2002.

T. Perkins, 'Plans for regional banks are a radical leap for Britain', Open Democracy website, 26 April 2013, [online], available at: http://www.opendemocracy.net/ourkingdom/toby-perkins/plans-for-regional-banks-are-radical-leap-for-britain [Accessed 02/09/2013].

R. Peston, 'Should hedge funds be disenfranchised?', BBC online, 10 February 2010, available at: http://www.bbc.co.uk/blogs/thereporters/robertpeston/2010/02/should_hedge_funds_be_disenfra.html [Accessed: 02/09/2013].

J. Plender, *A Stake In the Future*, London: Nicholas Brierley Publishing, 1996.

J. Portes, 'Not the Treasury View', 21 December 2012, Blog Post from NIESR, available at: http://notthetreasuryview.blogspot.co.uk/ [Accessed: 02/09/2013].

R. Putnum, *Bowling Alone: The collapse and revival of American community*, New York: Simon & Schuster, 2002.

R. Rajan, *Faultlines*, Princeton: Princeton University Press, 2010.

A. Reece, 'Reviving British Manufacturing: Why? What? How?', *Civitas*, July 2011.

D. Rodrik, 'Normalising Industrial Policy', University of Harvard, September 2008.

J. Ross, 'The incredible shrinking UK economy', 15 January 2012, Blog Post from Key Trends in Globalisation, available at: http://ablog.typepad.com/keytrendsinglobalisation/2012/01/the-incredible-shrinking-uk-economy.html [Accessed: 02/09/2013].

D. Sainsbury, *Progressive Capitalism*, London: Biteback Books, 2013.

M. Sandel, 'How Markets Crowd Out Morals', *The Boston Review*, 1 May 2012.

A. Shonfield, *Modern Capitalism: The Changing Balance of Public and Private*, Oxford: Oxford University Press, 1965.

A. Sissons, 'Manu-services: best of both worlds', 23 October 2011, Work Foundation Blog Post, available at: http://www.theworkfoundation.com/blog/540/Manuservices-best-of-both-worlds [Accessed: 02/09/2013].

R. Skidelsky 'The relevance of Keynes', *Cambridge Journal of Economics*, Volume 35, issue 1, 17 January 2011, pp. 1-13.

G. Sperling, *The Pro-Growth Progressive: An Economic Strategy for Shared Prosperity*, New York: Simon & Schuster, 2005.

H. Steedman, '*The state of apprenticeship in 2010: international comparisons – Australia, Austria, England, France, Germany, Ireland, Sweden, Switzerland: a report for the Apprenticeship Ambassadors Network*', Centre for Economic Performance special papers, Centre for Economic Performance, London School of Economics and Political Science, 2010.

H. Stewart, K. Allen and N. Bunyan, 'Two-speed Britain as London soars away from the rest', *The Guardian,* 12 May 2013.

H. Thompson, 'No Way Back: The legacy of a financial sector debt crisis', Policy Network, 5 September 2012.

HM Treasury, 'The Plan for Growth', March 2011.

A. Turner, *Just Capital: The Liberal Economy*, London: Pan Books, 2002.

K. Ussher, 'What is Predistribution?', Policy Network, 12 October 2012.

N. Watt and J. Treanor, 'David Cameron raises prospect of 1980s-style RBS sell-off', *The Guardian,* 15 May 2013

M. Weale, 'Commentary: Growth Prospects and Financial Services', *National Institute Economic Review*, 207, 2009, pp. 3-9.

D. Wheldon, 'A Diverse Banking System', Fabian Society, 15th March 2013, [online] available at: http://www.fabians.org.uk/a-diverse-banking-system/ [Accessed 02/09/2013].

K. Williams, 'British industrial policy remains plagued by the antidote fallacy', *The Guardian*, 24 December 2012.

A. Wolf, 'Can we educate our way out of trouble?', University of Plymouth Lecture, 24 October 2012.

L. Young, 'Growing Your Business', May 2013, [online], available at: https://www.gov.uk/government/uploads/system/

uploads/attachment_data/file/198165/growing-your-business-lord-young.pdf [Accessed: 02/09/2013].